PEARSON

ALWAYS LEARNING

Practices of Instruction
Workbook

Third Custom Edition

Patrice LeBlanc, Ed.D
and Helena Clementi-Rozlivkova, Ph.D.

Cover Art: Matisse Dream, by George Herman.

Pearson Learning Solutions, 501 Boylston Street, Suite 900, Boston, MA 02116
A Pearson Education Company
www.pearsoned.com

Printed in the United States of America

1 2 3 4 5 6 7 8 9 10 VOCR 17 16 15 14 13

000200010271829898

MC

ISBN 10: 1-269-57867-7
ISBN 13: 978-1-269-57867-7

Table of Contents

Module 1
Introduction

Purpose of the Book

Greetings! We would like you to know that teacher candidates who have used the prior editions of this book have told us that it has served as a valuable resource for them. Our hope is that you find this new edition, *Practices of Instruction: Workbook*, an equally useful tool as you complete your teacher education program.

This new edition of the book has been developed with you in mind. In it you will find material presented in short, easy to read, bursts of information. There are lists, charts, graphic organizers, and activities designed to engage you in learning. There are also tips and tools for you to use when you teach students. In general, we chose to list all references and sources at the end of each module and not to cite within the text. In this way, we were able to streamline the visual representations of the material for you while still providing you with access to references and sources as appropriate.

The book is organized into twelve modules centered on assisting you with developing an effective lesson plan. Module 1 serves as an introduction by providing background information: a conceptual model of the instructional cycle, some ideas for field experiences, the standard lesson plan format, and information on study skills for you and your future students.

The subsequent modules focus on the various parts of the lesson plan. Module 2 discusses context for the lesson plan, and Module 3 addresses lesson plan materials. Module 4 describes things teachers do to motivate students and engage them in learning. Module 5 introduces lesson plan content, grade level expectations, and standards. How to write goals and objectives is discussed in Module 6. In Module 7, instructing students from special populations is examined. Module 8 presents information related to the six universal pedagogical models for instruction used from prekindergarten through graduate school. Module 9 provides some tips for classroom management. In Module 10, ways to monitor and assess students' learning are reviewed. Module 11 gives tips for closing a lesson. The final module, Module 12, describes teacher reflection.

We sincerely hope that this new edition of the book assists you in your development toward teacher effectiveness by adding to your best practices. We wish you success in your career goals!

Patrice LeBlanc and Helena Clementi-Rozlivkova

The Instructional Cycle

**Plan
Instruction**

**Assess
Instruction**

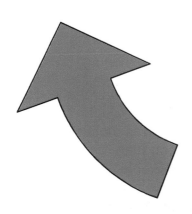

Instruct

The Instructional Cycle depicts
the step-by-step teaching process
teachers routinely use
in order to increase student learning.

Lesson Plan Writing Guide

I. General Information

> **What It Is**
> ❖ **General information** includes things such as:
> - the grade level and age of the students,
> - the subject area taught,
> - the title of the lesson, and
> - the lesson's duration (i.e., time needed to teach it).
>
> **Rationale for It**
> ✓ This information orients the cooperating teacher and your instructor.

II. Context

> **What It Is**
> ❖ **Context** refers to the:
> - gender,
> - race,
> - ethnicity, and
> - special populations (e.g., English Speakers of Other Languages, Special Education, Remedial, etc.) of your students.
>
> **Rationale for It**
> ✓ Knowing this information enables you to plan your lesson to meet the diverse needs of your students.

III. Instructional Materials

> **What They Are**
> ❖ In this section you identify the **materials** or learning resources you will use when teaching. Examples are
> - traditional materials (e.g., textbooks, workbooks and/or worksheets, science equipment, fractions tiles, etc.) and
> - technological materials (e.g., websites, videos/video clips, Power Point presentations, etc.).
>
> **Rationale for Them**
> ✓ To motivate and engage students in learning, a variety of materials are needed.
> ✓ Also, listing what materials you will use when teaching will help you stay organized as you prepare to teach your lesson.

IV. Set

What It Is

❖ **Set** is a term used to describe what you will do to catch students' attention and motivate them to learn. The tools for set include but are not limited to:
- telling students what they are about to learn,
- making statements to connect the goal of the lesson to students' prior knowledge of the content,
- using a variety of materials, and
- sharing experiences to engage students' interest in the lesson.

Rationale for It

✓ Using set enhances students' learning by helping them make cognitive connections with past learning, motivating them to continue learning, and engaging them in instruction.

V. Content, Grade Level Expectations, and Standards

What They Are

❖ **Content** refers to the subject area and topic you will teach.

❖ **Grade level expectations** are located in your state's standards.

❖ State **standards** identify the scope and sequence of the content to be taught in your state. In Florida the standards are called Collaborate, Plan, Align, Learn, Motivate, and Share (CPALMS). These standards have been undergoing revision, and you will find the most current version at the Department of Education website (http://www.cpalms.org/homepage/index.aspx).

Rationale for Them

✓ Since all teachers must teach to the state standards for their state, identifying these standards is a requirement.

✓ The standards at a given grade level reflect the expectations for students at that level.

✓ As a teacher, you must teach the content to prepare students for the state assessment test. In Florida, this test is called the Florida Comprehensive Assessment Test (FCAT).

VI. Goal

What It Is
* A **goal** is a broad statement that describes the overall aim of your lesson.
* When writing a goal, make sure that it **echoes the standards** your lesson addresses.
* Also, make sure that you know how the goal **fits with other lessons** in the subject area and topic that were previously taught and what will be taught in the future.

Rationale for It
✓ Having a goal helps you in planning because it provides you with the general aim of your lesson, incorporates the standards you must cover, and demonstrates the fit with previous and subsequent lessons.

VII. Objectives

What They Are
* **Objectives** are specific short statements that clarify what you want your students to know and be able to do after completing the lesson.
Well written objectives meet the following criteria:
  * sequenced according to the learning domain (i.e., cognitive, affective, psychomotor),
  * consistent in content,
  * written in observable terms,
  * fit with the selected standards and goals, and
  * promote the continuous development of each student (e.g., cognitive: critical thinking, problem solving; affective: collaboration, respect; psychomotor: coordination, stamina).

Rationale for Them
✓ Objectives guide your lesson by providing a sequenced list of the things that you want your students to know and be able to do. Thus, the objectives can help you determine the variety of materials and activities you will use to help students develop their knowledge and skills.

VIII. Accommodations

What They Are

❖ **Accommodations** are ways in which you change students' instruction to enable students with diverse needs to meet the lesson objectives. Accommodations include things such as:

- using multi-sensory strategies when teaching,
- presenting content-based vocabulary, and
- modifying activities and assignments.

Rationale for Them

✓ In order to meet the learning needs of all children, effective teachers make accommodations in the teaching-learning process that enable all children to learn. In fact, there are laws and court decisions that require teachers to accommodate the needs of ESOL and ESE learners.

IX. Instruction

What It Is

❖ **Instruction** refers to the method, or step-by-step process, that you will use to teach your students your lesson so that they meet the lesson's objectives.

❖ Specifically, you need to identify which **model** (i.e., presentation, concept teaching, direct instruction, cooperative learning, problem-based instruction, or discussion) or combination of strategies from the models (e.g., advance organizers, graphic organizers, chunking, etc.) you will use in the lesson.

❖ You also need to describe the **teacher behaviors** you will use when teaching (e.g., marker expressions, movement around the classroom, etc.).

❖ Finally, instruction also includes the **student activities** you will use to assist your students with meeting the objectives. Remember, student activities are what the students do during the lesson.

Rationale for It

✓ Research in the field of education (see Arends, 2012) provides evidence that the teaching models and strategies are effective ways to insure that students learn the lesson's objectives.

X. Classroom Management

XI. Monitoring

XII. Assessment

> **What It Is**
> ❖ **Assessment** is how you know that your students have learned what you want them to know and be able to do by the end of the lesson. Assessment allows you to determine if the students have met the lesson's objectives.
> ❖ **Formative assessments** provide information about how the students' knowledge is progressing and, therefore, help you plan your future lessons. **Summative assessments** provide information about the students' achievement and allow you to make judgments about that achievement (e.g., grades).
> ❖ Assessment can be **traditional**, such as paper and pencil tasks or recitation. Assessment can be **alternative**, such as performance or alternative assessment.
> ❖ It is also important to note any **assessment accommodations** that you will make in order to insure that your assessments are suitable for students with diverse needs.
> **Rationale for It**
> ✓ By assessing students' learning, you are able to ascertain that what you are teaching is being learned by the students. In this way, you can determine students' achievement to ensure that they have met the grade level standards.

XIII. Closure

> **What It Is**
> ❖ All things have a beginning and an end. Set is the beginning of your lesson while **closure** is the end of your lesson.
> ❖ Closure ends the lesson by briefly reviewing the material that was just covered. It is important to involve students in this end of lesson **review**.
> ❖ It is also important to help students make connections to future lessons. Some ways to **promote connections** are activities that extend thinking (e.g., reviewing a completed advance organizer, assigning homework on the topic, recommending family activities on the topic, etc.).
> **Rationale for It**
> ✓ Closing the lesson provides a summary of learning for students and enables them to make higher level cognitive connections thereby enhancing their academic achievement.

XIV. Reflections

What It Is

❖ **Reflection** in teaching is when you conduct a self-assessment of your planning and instruction of the lesson. In essence, you think about the lesson that you have just taught, identifying what was successful so that you can repeat it and evaluating what needs to be improved and why so that you are more effective in your instruction.

Rationale for It

✓ Reflective practitioners are able to improve their teaching based upon their reflections. They strive for teaching effectiveness.

Note: The sections of this generic lesson plan are adapted from the required lesson plan template for the Nova Southeastern University Teacher Education Program. The template was developed by faculty at a Curriculum Retreat in May of 2012.

Activities for Field Experiences

Field experiences refer to the opportunities teacher candidates have to observe teachers and work with students in live classrooms or in virtual ones. The goals of field experiences are for you to: (1) gain experience with the everyday operations of the classroom and (2) practice your newly learned teaching skills. The following list suggests a variety of activities in order to help you meet these goals.

I. Classroom Management and Housekeeping

- ✓ Greet students at the door to the classroom.
- ✓ Take attendance.
- ✓ Collect forms and money from students.
- ✓ Facilitate the passing and collection of papers and worksheets.
- ✓ Facilitate students lining up for movement to another location.
- ✓ Monitor students walking to other classrooms, lunch, and/or recess.
- ✓ Do lunch, recess, or dismissal duty.

II. Instruction and Assessment

- ✓ Create a bulletin board.
- ✓ Make graphic organizers.
- ✓ Write assignments on the board.
- ✓ Set up manipulatives and/or experiments for lessons.
- ✓ Correct papers.
- ✓ Check homework.
- ✓ Help students locate library books.
- ✓ Monitor seat work.
- ✓ Monitor small group work.
- ✓ Assist students individually.
- ✓ Help an ESOL student.
- ✓ Work with a disabled student.
- ✓ Teach a small group of students.
- ✓ Read a story to the class.
- ✓ Identify and present multimedia activities to support a lesson.
- ✓ Teach a whole class lesson.
- ✓ Give a quiz, test, or alternative assessment.
- ✓ Observe a parent-teacher conference.
- ✓ Observe an Individualized Educational Plan meeting.

Module 1.5
Study Skills

Tips for Study Skills

Courtesy of Fotolia

Steps for Completing Assignments

Step 1
Determine the intention of the assignment.

Step 2
Identify the question or problem you must address to complete the assignment.

Step 3
Determine the knowledge you need to answer the question or problem.

Step 4
Apply frameworks, theories, or principles to help you answer the question or problem.

Step 5
Generate answers or solutions for the question or problem.

Strategies for Studying

1. Organize
   A. Format information using an outline.
   B. Use a content analysis of generalizations, concepts, and facts.
   C. Create concept maps or maps of facts.
   D. Use chunking by splitting the material into conceptual groupings to make manageable amounts.

2. Elaborate
   A. Survey, question, read, record, recite, and review (SQ4R).
   B. Read and take notes on paper, note cards, or computer.
   C. Make analogies or metaphors for important facts.

3. Rehearse
   A. Memorize facts (e.g., oral repetition, flashcards, mnemonics, acronyms, link).
   B. Underline or highlight when reading.
   C. Take notes in the margins when reading.

4. Metacognitive Strategies
   A. Scaffold your learning by joining a study group.
   B. Use cognitive monitoring by constantly checking your own learning.

Tips for Developing a Content Analysis

I. Definitions

A. What is a content analysis?

- ✓ A **content analysis** reorganizes textual material.
- ✓ It provides a framework for thinking about and studying that text.
- ✓ It is composed of three levels: generalizations, concepts, and facts.

B. What is a generalization?

- ✓ A **generalization** is a broad synthesizing statement that encompasses several concepts.
- ✓ Usually, the generalization can be stated in one sentence. However, if there is a lot of information related to the generalization, several sentences may be needed.

C. What is a concept?

- ✓ A **concept** is a statement of an important idea.
- ✓ It includes the term or concept label and the definition of it.
- ✓ A concept is written in sentence format.

D. What is a fact?

- ✓ A **fact** is a piece of information that can be verified as reality or truth.
- ✓ It is not an opinion, but may be a piece of information that is stated in the form of a theory.
- ✓ A fact is written as a phrase.

II. Making a Content Analysis

A. What steps do you follow to make a content analysis?

1. Start with the first generalization.
2. Then, identify the first concept related to it, and place the concept underneath the generalization.
3. Next, place the facts related to the first concept underneath it.
4. Repeat the concept-facts process for each concept related to the first generalization.
5. Then, repeat the whole generalization-concepts-facts process with each subsequent generalization.

B. How do you organize a content analysis?

1. Put your generalization at the top and work downward on the document, so your analysis is presented in a sequential manner.
2. Remember that a content analysis in this format is deductive in nature, meaning that it starts with the general rules and ideas that lead to the facts or examples.
3. Make sure that each generalization is supported by concepts, and each concept is supported by facts.

C. How do you make a content analysis clear?

1. When there is a large amount of material, use sub-concepts and/or sub-facts to keep the information organized.
2. Use roman numerals, numbers, and letters, as you would in an outline to bring greater clarity to your content analysis.
3. Use different colored font or underline important ideas and/or terms.
4. Indenting each level of your content analysis helps with organization as well (e.g., generalization at the margin, concepts indent a half inch, facts indent an inch).

D. How do you cite and reference the contents of the analysis?

1. As you paraphrase, insert the citation (e.g., LeBlanc & Clementi-Rozlivkova, 2014).
2. As you quote, use "quotation marks" and insert the citation (e.g., LeBlanc & Clementi-Rozlivkova, 2014, p. 14).
3. Remember to list the full American Psychological Association reference at the end of your content analysis to denote the source of your work.

Sample Content Analysis

Standard

Content: social studies

Grade Level: 4

Strand: American History

Standard: Exploration and settlement of Florida

Benchmark Number: SS.4.A.3.2

Benchmark Description: Describe causes and effects of European colonization on the Native American tribes of Florida

(FL DOE, 2012)

Content Analysis of the Causes and Effects of European Colonization on the Native American Tribes of Florida

Generalization 1

Wealth and **religion** were the causes for European colonization of the Native American tribes of Florida.

Concept 1.1

Europeans wanted to trade in order to become **rich** and **powerful**.

Facts

1. Europeans' search for easier trade routes brought them to Florida.
2. Juan Ponce de Leon searched for the Fountain of Youth.
3. Other Florida explorers searched for gold.
4. Conquistadors established colonies to acquire more land for Spain making Spain more powerful.
5. Spain traded for the natural resources in Florida.
6. Native Americans traded for crops, animals, and weapons.

Concept 1.2

Europeans wanted to convert others to the Christian **religion** or practice their own religion freely.

Facts

1. The Spanish built missions that included churches in order to teach the Native Americans about Christianity and Spanish life.
2. The French came to Florida to practice their own religion freely.

Generalization 2

The effects of European colonization on the Native American tribes of Florida were changes in "**culture**", "**agriculture**", "**conflict**", "**disease**", and "**slavery**" (Banks, et al., 2013, pp. 73-75).

Concept 2.1

The European colonization of Florida **changed the culture** of Native Americans.

Facts

1. At the missions, many Native Americans converted to Christianity.
2. Native Americans learned how to dress like the Spanish.
3. Native Americans learned the Spanish language.

Concept 2.2

The European colonization of Florida **changed agriculture** of Native Americans.

Facts

1. Europeans brought new crops, such as "oranges", "watermelons, peaches, peas, wheat, and garbanzo beans" to the Native Americans (Banks, et al., p. 73).
2. Europeans brought new animals, such as "cattle", "pigs, chickens, sheep, goats, and horses" to the Native Americans (Banks, et al., p. 73).

Concept 2.3

The European colonization of Florida brought **conflict, disease, and slavery** to Native Americans.

Facts

1. Europeans and Native Americans fought over the land.
2. Native Americans lost many of the fights; they died or had to move to new land.
3. Europeans exposed Native Americans to diseases like measles and small pox; many Native Americans died.

4. Some Europeans forced Native Americans to become slaves.

5. Some Native Americans were required to work in the missions.

References

Banks, J. A., Colleary, K. P., Greenow, L., Parker, W. C., Schell, E. M., and Zike, D., Denham, J. M., Leonard, M. C. B., McTighe, J., & Shanahan, T. (2013). *Florida social studies: Florida studies. Unit two: Exploration and colonization of Florida.* NY, NY: McGraw-Hill.

Florida Department of Education (FL DOE). (2012). *Collaborate, plan, learn, motivate, and share (CPALMS): Standards.* Retrieved from http://www.cpalms.org/standards/flstandardsearch.aspx

Tips for Developing a Concept Map

I. Definitions

A. What is a concept map?

- ✓ A **concept map** reorganizes textual material.
- ✓ It provides a framework for thinking about and studying that text.
- ✓ Typically, the map presents the concepts covered in the text and indicates relationships among those concepts.

B. What is a concept?

- ✓ A **concept** is a statement of an important idea.
- ✓ It includes the term or concept label and the definition of it.

C. What is a relationship?

- ✓ A **relationship** between or among concepts indicates how the concepts are connected conceptually.
- ✓ These conceptual relationships may include various types, such as a concept with examples and non-examples, cause and effect, a rule and its application, or a value judgment and its justification.

II. Making a Concept Map

A. What steps do you follow to make a concept map?

1. To create your concept map, start by identifying all the key concepts in the text.

2. Next, examine the relationships between or among concepts.

3. Decide which concept and relationship are the focus of your lesson and place that concept at the top of the map in a balloon or box.

4. Then, place the other concepts—either in a clockwise fashion or top to bottom and left to right—in other balloons or boxes.

5. Draw lines connecting concepts to show evidence of relationships.

6. Add phrases to describe the conceptual relationships.

B. How do you organize a concept map?

1. As stated above, work either in a clockwise fashion or top to bottom and left to right so that your students can follow the concepts and their relationships as they read downward from the top of the map.

2. Remember that concept maps are deductive in nature, so make sure that each concept and its relationships are clearly indicated.

C. How do you make a concept map clear?

1. Remember to start at the top and work downward, so your map is presented in a sequential manner.
2. Use roman numerals, numbers, and letters to identify the sequence of concepts and relationships.
3. Use different colored font or underline important ideas and/or terms.

D. How do you cite and reference the contents of the map?

1. As you paraphrase, insert the citation (e.g., LeBlanc & Clementi-Rozlivkova, 2014).
2. As you quote, use "quotation marks" and insert the citation (e.g., LeBlanc & Clementi-Rozlivkova, 2014, p. 14).
3. Remember to list the full American Psychological Association reference at the end of your content analysis to denote the source of your work.

Sample Concept Map

Standard
Content: social studies
Grade Level: 4
Strand: American History
Standard: Exploration and settlement of Florida
Benchmark Number: SS.4.A.3.2
Benchmark Description: Describe causes and effects of European colonization on the Native American tribes of Florida
(FL DOE, 2012)

Content Analysis of the Causes and Effects of European Colonization on the Native American Tribes of Florida

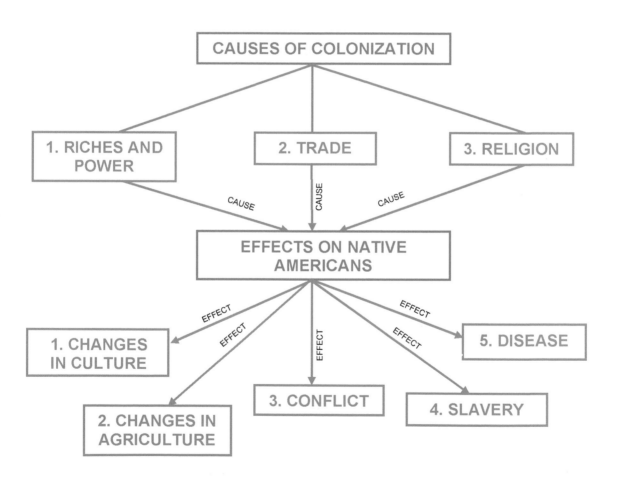

Note: The content in this concept map is drawn from Banks, et al. (2012).

References

Banks, J. A., Colleary, K. P., Greenow, L., Parker, W. C., Schell, E. M., and Zike, D., Denham, J. M., Leonard, M. C. B., McTighe, J., & Shanahan, T. (2013). *Florida social studies: Florida studies. Unit two: Exploration and colonization of Florida.* NY, NY: McGraw-Hill.

Florida Department of Education (FL DOE). (2012). *Collaborate, plan, learn, motivate, and share (CPALMS): Standards.* Retrieved from http://www.cpalms.org/standards/flstandardsearch.aspx

1.5.5

Activity 1: Creating a Content Analysis

Directions:

Review the information in this module; then, complete the items below. Remember to submit the final product to your instructor on the due date.

1. In this activity you are to select a student textbook from the field experiences classroom in which you are placed this term. If you are an Elementary Education or Special Education major, the text should be social studies or science.

2. Select a chapter to read.

3. Go to the standards for your state and identify the standards that are covered in the chapter. Knowing the standards will help you to identify the generalizations, concepts, and facts.

4. Read the chapter.

5. Decide what generalizations, concepts, and facts are covered in the chapter.

6. Create a content analysis handout for students as a document that you can save on your computer. Use the directions in Module 1.5.2 to assist you.

7. Review and edit your assignment for clarity, accuracy, grammar, and mechanics.

8. Be sure to cite and reference your work.

Activity 2: Creating a Concept Map

Directions:

Review the information in this module; then, complete the items below. Remember to submit the final product to your instructor on the due date.

1. In this activity you will use the same student textbook that you used for Activity 1. In this way, you will have an opportunity to practice another way to present the same material to your students to enhance their learning.
2. Reread the chapter.
3. Review the standards that are covered in the chapter.
4. Review what concepts are covered in the chapter.
5. Create a concept map handout for students as a document that you can save on your computer. Consider using Microsoft Word graphics or a graphics program. Use the directions from Module 1.5.4 to assist you.
6. Review and edit your assignment for clarity, accuracy, grammar, and mechanics.
7. Be sure to cite and reference your work.

Module 1 References and Sources

Arends, R. I. (2012). *Learning to teach* (9th ed.). New York: McGraw-Hill.

Banks, J. A., Colleary, K. P., Greenow, L., Parker, W. C., Schell, E. M., & Zike, D., Denham, J. M., Leonard, M. C. B., McTighe, J., & Shanahan, T. (2013). *Florida social studies: Florida studies. Unit two: Exploration and colonization of Florida.* NY, NY: McGraw-Hill.

Borich, G. D. (2014). *Effective teaching methods* (8th ed.). Upper Saddle River, NJ: Pearson.

Burden, P. R., & Byrd, D. M. (2013). *Methods for effective teaching: Meeting the needs of all students* (6th ed.). Boston: Allyn & Bacon.

Estes, T. H., Mintz, S. L., & Gunter, M. A., (2011). *Instruction: A models approach* (6th ed.) Upper Saddle River, NJ: Pearson.

Florida Department of Education (FL DOE). (2012). *Collaborate, plan, learn, motivate, and share (CPALMS): Standards.* Retrieved from http://www.cpalms.org/standards/flstandardsearch.aspx

LeBlanc, P., & Clementi-Rozlivkova, H. (2014). *Practices of instruction: Workbook* (3rd ed.). Upper Saddle River, NJ: Pearson Custom Publishing.

Morrison, G. R., Ross, S. M., Kalman, H., & Kemp, J. E. (2013). *Designing effective instruction* (6th ed.). Indianapolis, IN: John Wiley & Sons.

Paul, R., & Elder, L. (2013). *Critical thinking concepts framework.* Retrieved from http://louisville.edu/ideastoaction/about/criticalthinking/framework

Module 2
Context

The Importance of Knowing Context

What is context?

Context refers to the background of the students in your classroom, and the students in 21st century classrooms have very diverse backgrounds.

Courtesy of Fotolia

For example, the students in your classroom will come from different home environments that impact who they are as people and how they learn. Some students will come from affluent families with many material items, while others may come from homes where they don't have enough to eat. Students' **socioeconomic status** has an impact on their everyday exposure to knowledge and may impact their learning in the classroom.

Another area of diversity is **family structure**. Some students may live with two biological parents or foster parents or a single parent, while others may spend part of their time with each divorced parent. Students may live with grandparents or with one divorced parent who has remarried. Students may be only children, have siblings, or have half-brothers and/or half-sisters. Today's families are diverse in make-up and understanding that there is no, one, right type of family is an important part of accepting your students. However, this variation may mean that some of your students will be coping with changes in their family structure, which may influence their learning in the classroom.

Courtesy of Fotolia

Courtesy of Fotolia

Also, the students in your classroom will be diverse in their **races, ethnicities, languages, religions, cultures, and learning abilities**. As a teacher, you will need to understand, accept, and respect the diversity of each child in your classroom. Activities that promote students' understanding of each other and teaching them to accept and respect each other will create a caring climate in your classroom that will support learning. Also, you will need to **adapt lessons to accommodate students' diverse needs** to ensure their success.

Knowing as much information as possible about your students (without violating their privacy) will help you in your lesson planning and instruction!

Activity 3: Selecting a Student Interest Inventory

What Is a Student Interest Inventory?

A **student interest inventory** is a printed series of questions that students answer thoughtfully. The questions cover a variety of information about students but have a particular focus on what their interests are. As a teacher, you can develop your own inventory or use one of the many printable inventories available on the web. Knowing about students' interests will provide you with context information for your lesson planning.

Directions:

Review the information in this module; then, complete the items below.

1. Do a **web search** for student interest inventories. (Two popular ones are listed on the *Module 2 References and Sources* page.)

2. Review some inventories designed for the **grade level of your field experiences** placement.

3. **Review the questions** on the inventories to ensure that they gather useful information.

4. **Select** a student interest inventory as it is, or create one of your own based on your review of several inventories. Remember to **cite and reference** the inventory.

5. If you are taking a course with field experiences this term, **print** enough copies of the student interest inventory for your field experiences class.

6. **Administer** the student interest inventory to your field experiences class.

7. Share the results with your cooperating teacher and **use the information to assist you with the context for your lesson planning.**

Module 2 References and Sources

Arends, R. I. (2012). *Learning to teach* (9th ed.). New York: McGraw-Hill.

Banks, J. A. (2014). *An introduction to multicultural education* (5th ed.). Upper saddle River, NJ: Pearson.

Borich, G. D. (2014). *Effective teaching methods* (8th ed.). Upper Saddle River, NJ: Pearson.

Burden, P. R., & Byrd, D. M. (2013). *Methods for effective teaching: Meeting the needs of all students* (6th ed.). Upper Saddle River, NJ: Pearson.

Estes, T. H., Mintz, S. L., & Gunter, M. A., (2011). *Instruction: A models approach* (6th ed.) Upper Saddle River, NJ: Pearson.

Nieto, S., & Bode, P. (2012). *Affirming diversity: The sociopolitical context of multicultural education* (6th ed.). Upper Saddle Rive, NJ: Pearson.

Scholastic Printables. (2013). *Student interest inventory questionnaire.* Scholastic, Inc. Retrieved from http://printables.scholastic.com/printables/detail/?id=35571

Sanchez, M. (2003). *Student interest inventory.* Retrieved from www.sanchezclass.com/docs/student-interest-inventory.pdf

Module 3
Instructional Materials

Identifying Appropriate Instructional Materials

Introduction

To identify appropriate instructional materials, you should consider the following areas. First, identify what materials you will use for the various parts of the lesson/unit plan, being sure to use both traditional and technological materials. Second, select instructional materials that will help your students meet the standards and objectives of your lesson. Third, be sure that the material is age/grade appropriate. Fourth, consider the usability of the materials: ensure that they are easily accessed/handled by you and the students; their use fits the time frame of your lesson/unit; and they are low cost but high quality. Fifth, use a variety of materials within a lesson to catch your students' attention and enhance their motivation for learning. Also, vary your materials to help address your students' learning styles and accommodate the needs of special populations. These areas for consideration have been listed as questions below to help you quickly and efficiently select your materials. Examples of technological and traditional materials follow.

Six Questions for Identifying Appropriate Instructional Materials

1. What parts of the lesson/unit plan do the materials address?

2. Are the materials appropriate for the grade level?

3. How does the instructional material support attainment of your lesson/unit standards, goal, and objectives?

4. How usable are the materials?
   A. Are they easily accessed/handled by you and the students?
   B. Does their use fit the time frame of your lesson or unit?
   C. Are the materials low cost but high quality?

5. Will the instructional material catch your students' attention and maintain motivation?

6. Do you have a variety of materials that help you to address your students' learning styles and accommodate the needs of special populations?

Examples of Traditional Materials

Courtesy of Fotolia

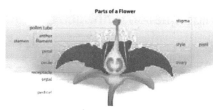

Courtesy of Fotolia

Courtesy of Fotolia

- Artwork (e.g., collages, comics, coloring, drawing, molding clay, painting, etc.)
- Educational games (e.g., Boggle, Hangman, etc.)
- Field trips
- Graphic organizers (e.g., concept maps, bar graphs, T-charts, timelines, Venn diagrams, etc.)
- Hands-on manipulatives (e.g., Cuisenaire rods, tangrams, play money, etc.)
- Projects (e.g., cooperative learning, individual)
- Movement (e.g., dances, exercises, games like Simon Says or Beach Ball, etc.)
- Music (e.g., playing musical instruments, rapping, singing, etc.)
- Posters
- Print books (e.g., autobiographies, biographies, histories, novels, plays, poetry, science, short stories, textbooks, etc.)
- Problem solving tasks
- Role plays
- Scavenger hunts
- Science experiments (e.g., growing plants, creating chemical changes, etc.)
- Slogans
- Worksheets (e.g., crosswords, drill and practice, fill-in-the-blank, Mad Libs, multiple choice, open ended questions, Suduko, word finds, etc.)
- Writing (e.g., journals, plays, short stories, etc.)

Examples of Technological Materials

Courtesy of Fotolia

Courtesy of Fotolia

- Animations
- Audio recordings (e.g., audio clips, iPods/Podcasts, etc.
- Blogs
- Computer applications/websites (e.g., Instagram, Facebook, Xtranormal, Google, Fotoflexer, Twitter, Facebook, Skype, Google+)
- Computerized educational games (see *Module 4 References and Sources* page for examples)
- E-books
- ELMO document camera
- Interactive white board
- Power Point/Slide Share
- Simulations
- Videos (e.g., films, remix videos, video clips, You Tube, etc.)
- Virtual manipulatives
- Web quests
- Wikis

Sample of Identifying Appropriate Instructional Materials for a Lesson/Unit

Introduction

This sample addresses the *Questions for Identifying Appropriate Instructional Materials* from Module 3.1. Please note that this sample is written with great detail to enhance your understanding of how to use the questions. When you complete the activity that asks you to identify appropriate instructional materials for your lesson, you are not required to provide the same amount of detail that is listed here. You may address the questions in the activity with a few bulleted items or brief sentences.

Sample

1. Parts of My Lesson/Unit Plan

Parts of the Unit Plan	Instructional Materials
Set	• remix video, computer, and projector
Accommodations: Content Area Vocabulary & Monitoring	• word bank worksheet • ELMO Document Camera • classroom web page • crossword puzzle in textbook
Instruction & Monitoring	• oral reading from textbook • recitation questions • T-chart • cooperative learning group project
Assessment	• teacher observation • word matching worksheet • Power Point slide on Slide Share • Florida Test Preparation Exercise from the textbook • Unit 2 Test from the textbook

Unit Standard

Content: social studies

Grade Level: 4

Strand: American History

Standard: Exploration and settlement of Florida

Benchmark Number: SS.4.A.3.2

Benchmark Description: Describe causes and effects of European colonization on the Native American tribes of Florida

(FL DOE, 2012)

My instructional materials support attainment of my unit standard (see above) because the materials present the required content and/or reinforce learning of the content identified in the standard.

Goal: Students will understand the causes of European colonization and the effects of that colonization on the Native American Tribes of Florida.

Objectives: The objectives for my unit and their connection to the materials follow.

1. The students will view a remix video on the causes and effects of European colonization on the Native American tribes of Florida to spark interest in the lesson, as measured by teacher observation.
2. The students will define the content vocabulary words related to the causes and effects of European colonization on the Native American tribes of Florida, as monitored by their performance on a word bank worksheet.
3. The students will practice the vocabulary words related to the causes and effects of European colonization on the Native American tribes of Florida, as monitored by their performance on a crossword puzzle.
4. The students will understand and apply the meanings of the vocabulary words related to the causes and effects of European colonization on the Native American tribes of Florida, as measured by their performance on a word matching worksheet.
5. The students will orally read, understand, search, analyze, and critique the content in the textbook related to the causes and effects of European colonization on the Native American tribes of Florida, as monitored by recitation questions and the T-chart and assessed by their performance on the Unit 2 test.
6. The students will engage in a cooperative learning group project in order to locate, discuss, exhibit, analyze, and critique information about Florida Explorers that relates to the causes and effects of European colonization on the Native American tribes of Florida, as assessed by the Power Point slides they compose summarizing the information and shared via Slide Share.

3. Grade Appropriate

Traditional Materials

The textbook and accompanying activities (i.e., reading, crossword puzzle, Florida Test Preparation Exercise, and the Unit 2 Test) (Banks et al., 2013) are at the fourth grade level, the grade for which my unit plan has been designed. The materials that I have made (i.e., T-chart, the word bank worksheet, and word matching worksheet) use the vocabulary from the book, so they are grade appropriate. The remix video utilizes video clips, photos, and slides that I created with grade appropriate vocabulary and language. I developed the recitation questions to monitor students' learning based on the content of the textbook; therefore, they are grade appropriate.

Technological Materials

I will be using the ELMO document camera to show some of the materials described previously. The students will be using Power Point for their cooperative learning group projects and posting the slides to Slide Share for the entire class to use. These technology tools are used frequently with fourth graders in my school. Also, the classroom webpage is another tool used in my school. Teachers post self-developed materials on the page, as well as other items for student and parent use. The work sheets that I created will be posted on the webpage.

4. Usability

The materials are easily accessed/handled by me and the students. Each student has their own textbook, and I have a teacher's edition. The worksheets that I made are easily used by students, as the format is simple and the directions are clear. The remix video is on the classroom website, so it is easily accessed by me for showing in the classroom, and students may view the video again at home to use as a study aide for the unit test. I use the ELMO document camera regularly; it's easy to use and readily available. Also, the students are familiar with Power Point and Slide Share, making these technological materials stress-free to use.

The materials fit the time frame of my unit. Some materials, such as the textbook and recitation questions, will be used for each lesson. Other materials will be used intermittently. The Power Point program and Slide Share will be used by students in cooperative learning groups each day during their cooperative learning time. The final sharing of the slides in Slide Share will be used during the class just prior to the Unit 2 Test, the latter of which will occur during the last lesson of the unit.

The cost of the materials is minimal. The textbooks are high quality and were purchased previously. The other technology tools were also pre-purchased by the school. The only cost for the materials is the copying and paper for the worksheets, which are also part of the regular school budget. However, in order to conserve paper, I will print the worksheets as double-sided sheets, unless doing so compromises the quality of the worksheets.

5. Attention and Motivation

The remix video will initially catch students' attention and help motivate them to learn the topic. Using a combination of technological and traditional materials will also help keep students' attention and motivate them. For example, the students enjoy completing crossword puzzles and T-charts, so these materials are motivating. Another example is the cooperative learning project, which allows students to use technology to learn about the content. Being able to create a Power Point slide and post it to Slide Share is also motivational, as students enjoy using the technology.

6. Variety of Materials
Traditional Materials

My unit incorporates a number of traditional materials so that I can address both auditory and visual learners. An example is the word bank worksheet that promotes vocabulary development, as the material is presented auditorally while students have the visual of the word bank worksheet in front of them and its projection via the ELMO projector. The word bank worksheet, crossword puzzle in the textbook, and word matching worksheet accommodate the needs of special populations because there are multiple sheets in order to reinforce learning. Additionally, all students may use these worksheets for study aids as they read the material, work in their cooperative learning groups, and study for the test.

Technological Materials

Multiple technological materials also address learning styles. Two examples follow: interactive learners' needs will be met with the group project; visual and auditory learners' needs will be met with the remix video.

References

Banks, J. A., Colleary, K. P., Greenow, L., Parker, W. C., Schell, E. M., and Zike, D., Denham, J. M., Leonard, M. C. B., McTighe, J., & Shanahan, T. (2013). *Florida social studies: Florida studies. Unit two: Exploration and colonization of Florida.* NY, NY: McGraw-Hill.

Florida Department of Education (FL DOE). (2012). *Collaborate, plan, learn, motivate, and share (CPALMS): Standards.* Retrieved from http://www.cpalms.org/standards/flstandardsearch.aspx

Activity 4: Identifying Appropriate Instructional Materials

Directions:

Review the information in this module; then, complete the items below. Be sure that you can answer each question and provide examples. The questions may be answered using bulleted items or a few sentences. You may use the back pages of the activity to write the answers. Or, you may type up the answers as a Microsoft Word file, print the page, and attach it to the activity. Remember to submit the final product to your instructor on the due date.

Questions for Identifying Appropriate Instructional Materials

1. What parts of the lesson/unit plan do the materials address?

2. How does the instructional material support attainment of your lesson standards, goals, and objectives?

3. Are the materials appropriate for the grade level?

4. How usable are the materials?

   A. Are easily accessed/handled by you and the students?

   B. Does their use fit the time frame of your lesson or unit?

   C. Are the materials low cost but high quality?

5. Will the instructional material catch your students' attention and maintain motivation?

6. Do you have a variety of materials that help you to address your students' learning styles and accommodate the needs of special populations?

7. Review and edit your assignment for clarity, accuracy, grammar, and mechanics.

8. Be sure to cite and reference your work.

Module 3 References and Sources

Arends, R. I. (2012). *Learning to teach* (9th ed.). New York: McGraw-Hill.

Banks, J. A., Colleary, K. P., Greenow, L., Parker, W. C., Schell, E. M., and Zike, D., Denham, J. M., Leonard, M. C. B., McTighe, J., & Shanahan, T. (2013). *Florida social studies: Florida studies. Unit two: Exploration and colonization of Florida.* NY, NY: McGraw-Hill.

Borich, G. D. (2014). *Effective teaching methods* (8th ed.). Upper Saddle River, NJ: Pearson.

Burden, P. R., & Byrd, D. M. (2013). *Methods for effective teaching: Meeting the needs of all students* (6th ed.). Upper Saddle River, NJ: Pearson.

Campbell, L., Campbell, B., & Dickinson, D. (2004). *Teaching and learning through multiple intelligences* (3rd ed.). Upper Saddle River, NJ: Pearson.

Estes, T. H., Mintz, S. L., & Gunter, M. A., (2011). *Instruction: A models approach* (6th ed.) Upper Saddle River, NJ: Pearson.

Florida Department of Education (FL DOE). (2012). *Collaborate, plan, learn, motivate, and share (CPALMS): Standards.* Retrieved from http://www.cpalms.org/standards/flstandardsearch.aspx

Knowledge Adventure, Inc. (2011). *KA.* [Online educational games.] Retrieved from http://www.knowledgeadventure.com/default.aspx

Learning Games for Kids, Inc. (2013). *Learning games for kids.* [Online educational games.] Retrieved from http://www.learninggamesforkids.com/

Morrison, G. R., Ross, S. M., Kalman, H:, & Kemp, J. E. (2013). *Designing effective instruction* (6th ed.). Indianapolis, IN: John Wiley & Sons.

Nobelprize.org. (n.d.). [Online educational games.] Retrieved from http://www.nobelprize.org/educational/

Pearson Education, Inc. (200-2013). *Funbrain.* [Online educational games.] Retrieved from http://www.funbrain.com/

Module 4
Motivating Students

Learning Styles

I. What are learning styles?

Learning styles are a student's preference for the way in which he or she learns; the styles are the way the student learns best. For example, a student may learn best visually and globally.

By understanding your students' learning styles, you can incorporate activities into your lessons that address these various styles. For example, you might present a graphic organizer (i.e., visual) that provides a broad overview of the material (i.e., global). As a result, students will be more motivated to learn because you will be presenting material in the way in which they learn best.

II. How is the information sensed?

Courtesy of Fotolia

Visually means learning through seeing via graphic images such as pictures, icons, or graphic organizers.

Courtesy of Fotolia

Auditorally means learning through hearing via spoken, audiotapes, or music.

Courtesy of Fotolia

Kinesthetically means learning through touching via assembling things, drawing, or manipulatives.

How is the information perceived?

Sensory means that the information is garnered with the senses (e.g., seeing, hearing, touching).

Courtesy of Fotolia

Intuitive means that the information is garnered through instinct and acumen.

Courtesy of Fotolia

III. How is the information organized?

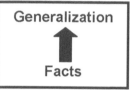

Generalization

↑

Facts

Inductive means working from the facts to the generalization, law or rule.

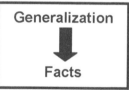

Generalization

↓

Facts

Deductive means working from the generalization, law or rule to the facts.

Also, information can be **understood and organized** two other ways.

Sequentially means that the information is viewed as a step-by-step process.

1, 2, 3, 4 . . .

Globally means that the information is viewed in total or as a whole.

Courtesy of Fotolia

IV. How is the information processed?

Courtesy of Fotolia

Deep processing means a search for the concepts and overall meaning of the material, as in the higher levels of the cognitive domain.

Courtesy of Fotolia

Surface processing means simple memorization, as in the first level of the cognitive domain.

Also, this **processing** can be conducted in either of two ways.

Actively means learning through participation in activities such as oral discussions, role-playing, or experiments.

Courtesy of Fotolia

Passively or **reflexively** means learning through a calm, deliberate, reasoned way.

Courtesy of Fotolia

For more information on learning styles, see the following websites.
http://www.nwlink.com/~donclark/hrd/styles.html
http://agelesslearner.com/intros/lstyleintro.html

For learning inventories to try on your own, see the following websites.
http://agelesslearner.com/assess/learningstyle.html
http://www.muskingum.edu/~cal/database/general/

Establishing Set

What is set?

Set means **getting the students set or ready to learn**. When you establish set, you present information that will entice the students to be interested in the lesson. Also, set can help students to think about the material that is about to be presented in the lesson at a higher level than the material itself, depending on the tool that you use to establish set. Next, when establishing set, you need to include a statement about the goal of the lesson. Be sure to connect that goal to students' prior knowledge of the content as well. Finally, remember that what you do must be brief but motivating!

To establish set, you may use a variety of tools. Some examples of these tools are listed here.

Tool	Example
Pose a question.	"Have you ever wondered why the moon appears to be a different size each night that it is visible? Today, we will be learning about the phases of the moon."
Present an advance organizer.	"As we go through this lesson on the food groups, think about whether or not you eat the recommended number of items for each food group daily."
Show a video clip, audio clip, or short remix video.	"Watch and listen to this video clip on volcanoes. We will be learning about what causes a volcano to erupt in this lesson."
Use a graphic organizer.	"Take a look at the graphic organizer. It's a character map. As we read through today's story, see if you can identify the characteristics of the characters and record them on the character map."
	"Today we will be learning about mammals. As we go through the lesson, we will be identifying the critical and noncritical attributes of a mammal. Use the T-chart to record the attributes."
	"In this lesson, I want you to think about what concepts fall into the center of the Venn diagram. These things are what the two categories have in common."

Advance Organizers

I. What are advance organizers?

> Advance organizers are an **aid for students' understanding of the material that is about to be taught** because they help to **consolidate the material**. Advance organizers are always presented at the beginning of the lesson, as they are used to help students think about the topic being presented at **a higher cognitive level** than the actual lesson material. As such, advance organizers promote students' development of higher level thinking. Advance organizers may be presented **auditorally, visually, or use both** learning styles.

II. Sample Advance Organizers

Here is an example of an advance organizer:

Example 1

Consider a lesson in which you are teaching facts about the Civil War (e.g., Many factories were built in the North. Northern factories sold their products to the Southerners. Southern farmers grew cotton. Southern cotton was sold to Northern factories.). For your advance organizer, you could pose a verbal statement such as: "As we go through the material in today's lesson, I want you to think about the facts, take notes about the facts, and determine how these facts might be categorized into concepts." (e.g., Differences between the Northern and Southern economies that influenced the outcome of the war). By asking your students to categorize the facts to determine concepts, they are required to use higher level thinking than simply recording facts.

Here are two suggestions for different advance organizers for another lesson:

Example 2

Think about a lesson in which you teach about environmental sustainability. You could make a verbal statement for your advance organizer: "As I present the facts about the environment, economy, and society to you, I want you to contrast and compare these facts. In particular, when you compare these facts, look for information about what makes a sustainable environment." This verbal advance organizer provides the concept (i.e., a sustainable environment) but requires students to contrast and compare facts related to the concept, which requires higher level thinking than simply recording facts.

Example 3

For a different advance organizer for this same lesson, you could use a graphic organizer (see Venn diagram below) with a verbal statement. You could tell the students: "On the Venn diagram, I want you to contrast the different facts for each area: environment, economy, and society by entering the facts in the appropriate circles. However, I also want you to compare the facts so that you can identify the similarities these three areas have in common. By doing so, you will answer the question: 'What makes a sustainable environment?'" This advance organizer requires the same higher level thinking as the previous example, but provides a visual representation to assist the students with their processing of the factual and conceptual information.

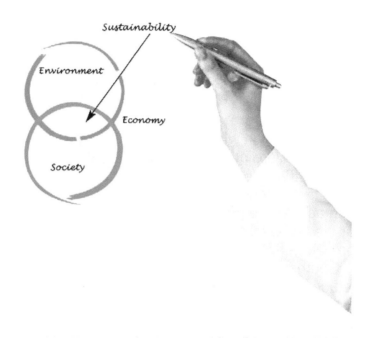

Courtesy of Fotolia

III. Conclusion

At the end of a lesson, you return to the advance organizer and ask the students to share what they learned. In this way, rather than simply teaching a lot of facts to be memorized, you will be helping the students to better remember the facts by having them consolidate the material and think about the information at a higher cognitive level.

Graphic Organizers

I. What are graphic organizers?

Graphic organizers are visuals that aid in students' understanding of the material being taught because they consolidate the material. Graphic organizers may also promote students' higher level thinking.

Graphic organizers can be created on the computer and posted to your classroom website. Students can then access, download, and save the documents for use on the computer or for printing. When your students don't have the availability of computers for use during your lesson, you will want to print and distribute the graphic organizers to the students so that the students can complete them in writing and/or take notes on them.

Below you will find some examples of graphic organizers and how to use them. To locate more types of graphic organizers along with downloadable samples, consider doing a web search for graphic organizers.

II. Examples of Graphic Organizers

Charts	Diagrams	Graphs	Maps	Tables
Continuum Chart	Character Traits diagram	Bar Graph	Chain Map	Five W's Table
Fishbone Chart	Cycle Diagram	Circle Graph	Cloud Map	Periodic Table
Flow Chart	Object Diagram	Line Graph	Concept Map	PMI Table
KWHL Chart	Spider Diagram	Timeline	Geographic Map	
Star Chart	Venn Diagram		Parts of the Plot Map	
Tree Chart				

III. Examples of How to Use Selected Graphic Organizers

Use a **KWHL Chart** before beginning a lesson/unit on a specific topic. It can be used to establish set for the lesson/unit, as an informal assessment, and as a way to review the topic for a formal assessment on the lesson/unit. A KWHL Chart has four columns in which you record students' answers to specific questions. Title the columns: **Know, Want, How, and Learn**. Complete the Know column by asking your students what information they already know about the topic of your lesson/unit and record it. To complete the Want column, probe your students to find out what they want to know about the topic and list the information in the column. Finish the How column by questioning your students about how they want to learn about the topic (e.g., group project, computer web quest). The completion of these first three columns can help you interest students in the topic and motivate them to learn, thereby establishing set. At the close of the lesson/unit, query the students about what they have learned about the topic and list the information in the Learn column. The Learn column of the graphic organizer can be used as a way to informally assess students' learning. Also, the completed KWHL Chart is a good way to review the topic with the students prior to a formal assessment.

You can use **Five W's Table** to promote students' thinking about a given topic. The Five W's Table is composed of five rows or boxes which begin with the questions: **who, what, when, where, and why**. To use this graphic organizer, you pose a question about the topic, and students complete the table by answering the question. For example the table is easily used for analysis of a story. Begin by asking, "Who is the main character in the story?" followed by "What was the most important thing that the main character in the story did?" Continue in this fashion, posing a question for each of the W's. By answering these five questions about a story, students can develop a deeper understanding of the story. Also, this graphic organizer can be used with a **Parts of the Plot Map**, where the students record the major parts of the plot using the information that they entered in the Five W's Table as a resource.

A **PMI Table** is used to help your students to help evaluate information on a specific topic. The table contains three columns labeled **Plus, Minus, and Implications**. To complete the Plus column, ask the students to identify positive things about the topic of the lesson/unit and record their answers. Next, ask the students to list the negative things about the topic and write them in the Minus column. For the Implications column, you and your students identify the implications of the items in the first two columns. You will write the implications in the column as conclusion statements or questions for further exploration. For example, for the topic of recycling, you might list the positive things about recycling (e.g., conserves resources), the negative ones (e.g., costly to collect and sort recyclables), and what the implications of these items are (e.g., Is conserving resources worth the cost?).

Connecting to Experiences

I. What is connecting to experiences?

> **Connecting to experiences** occurs when you or your students share real-life incidents that relate to the topic of lesson. For example, you or your students might verbally share a brief story, pictures, or video clips. In this way, a personal connection is made to the topic, which promotes interest and motivation to learn.
>
> Connecting to experiences is a technique that can be used at any point in the lesson. This strategy can establish set, illustrate a concept, or reinforce learning.

II. How to Connect to Experiences

One way to connect to experiences is to share an appropriate experience from your life. For example, you might be teaching a math lesson on adding and subtracting money. You could share a brief story about how, one time when you were a clerk in a convenience store, the power went out. The store remained open even though the cash register didn't calculate, but you could open the drawer with the money. So, you had to total the purchases, collect the money, and make accurate change for the people who were buying things in the store without relying on the cash register to add and subtract for you. You could close the story by telling the students: "Imagine what would have happened if I didn't know how to add and subtract money!" This story may catch the students' interest and motivate them to learn while illustrating the importance of the lesson topic.

Another way to connect to experiences is to involve students' experiences in the lesson. For the example lesson above, you might ask the students if their parents or guardians have ever let them purchase things in a store and pay the cashier themselves. You could call on one or two students to share what they bought, how much it cost, and how much change they received. You could write down what the students say to create sample math problems with adding and subtracting money, thereby connecting the topic to their personal experiences.

Courtesy of Fotolia

Activity 5: Comparing Advance and Graphic Organizers

Directions:

Review the information in this module; then, complete the items below. Remember to submit the final product to your instructor on the due date.

1. Draw a box around the words that indicate the | similarities | between the two methods.

2. Underline the words that indicate the **differences** between the two methods.

Advance Organizer	Graphic Organizer
Presented at the beginning of the lesson, used during the lesson, and reviewed at the end of the lesson	Presented at any point during the lesson, used at any point during the lesson, and reviewed at the end of the lesson
Is presented in verbal or visual format	Is presented in visual format
Provides a framework or structure for thinking about and/or organizing content that is about to be presented	Provides a framework or structure for thinking about and/or organizing content that is presented at any time
Challenges students to learn the content about to be presented at a higher cognitive level (e.g., asks for a higher level of thinking about the material rather than just comprehension)	Assists students in learning the content being presented

Activity 6: Practicing Set and Selecting a Graphic Organizer

Directions:

Review the information presented in this module and in Module 3. Then, complete the two items below. Remember to submit the final product to your instructor on the due date.

Item 1 – Set

A. Identify what you will say and do to establish set with your students for your lesson. If you are using a verbal statement, include a script of it. If you are using a graphic organizer, include a copy as part of this assignment.

B. Explain in a short paragraph why you have made your choice (i.e., answer the *Questions for Selecting Appropriate Instructional Materials* in Module 3.).

C. Review and edit your assignment for clarity, accuracy, grammar, and mechanics.

D. Be sure to cite and reference your work.

Item 2 – Graphic Organizer

A. Select one graphic organizer that you will use for your lesson and include a copy of it as part of this assignment.

B. Explain in a short paragraph why you have made your choice (i.e., answer the *Questions for Selecting Appropriate Instructional Materials* in Module 3.).

C. Review and edit your assignment for clarity, accuracy, grammar, and mechanics.

D. Be sure to cite and reference your work.

Module 4 References and Sources

Arends, R. I. (2012). *Learning to teach* (9th ed.). New York: McGraw-Hill.

Borich, G. D. (2014). *Effective teaching methods* (8th ed.). Upper Saddle River, NJ: Pearson.

Burden, P. R., & Byrd, D. M. (2013). *Methods for effective teaching: Meeting the needs of all students* (6th ed.). Boston: Allyn & Bacon.

Clark, D. (200-2012). *Learning styles and preferences.* A Big Dog, Little Dog and Knowledge Jump Production. Retrieved from http://www.nwlink.com/~donclark/hrd/styles.html

Clark, D. (200-2012). *Metalearning.* A Big Dog, Little Dog and Knowledge Jump Production. Retrieved from http://www.nwlink.com/~donclark/hrd/styles.html

Conner, M. (n.d.). *Informal learning, experiential learning, adult learning, and learning styles.* Retrieved from http://agelesslearner.com/intros/lstyleintro.html

Conner, M. (n.d.). *Learning inventories.* Retrieved from http://agelesslearner.com/intros/lstyleintro.html

edHelper.com. (n.d.). *Graphic organizers.* Retrieved from http://edhelper.com/teachers/graphic_organizers.htm

Education Place. (n.d.). *Graphic organizers.* Houghton-Mifflin Harcourt. Retrieved from http://www.eduplace.com/graphicorganizer/

Enchanted Learning.com. (n.d.). *Graphic organizer worksheets.* Retrieved from http://www.enchantedlearning.com/graphicorganizers/

Estes, T. H., Mintz, S. L., & Gunter, M. A., (2011). *Instruction: A models approach* (6th ed.) Upper Saddle River, NJ: Pearson.

Gardner, H. (2011). *Frames of mind: The theory of multiple intelligences.* NY, NY: Basic Books.

Morrison, G. R., Ross, S. M., Kalman, H., & Kemp, J. E. (2013). *Designing effective instruction* (6th ed.). Indianapolis, IN: John Wiley & Sons.

Muskingum University. (n.d.). *Learning strategies database.* Retrieved from http://www.muskingum.edu/~cal/database/general/

Woolfolk, A. (2014). *Educational psychology: Active learning edition* (12th ed.). Upper Saddle River, NJ: Pearson.

Module 5
Content, Grade Level
Expectations, and Standards

Connecting Content, Grade Level Expectations, and Standards

I. Terms

> **Content** is the material or information that you will teach. It is generally classified by subject area, category, and term or concept.

> **Grade level expectations** refer to what students should know and be able to do for their grade. For example, third graders are expected to know and use the math facts of multiplication and division; first graders are not expected to know this content.

> **Standards** combine the content and grade level expectations for each grade and identify the minimum level of knowledge that each student should be taught for that grade level. These standards may be at the state or national level.

> The **scope** of the content is how extensively or deeply the content is taught. Knowing how deeply to cover the material will help to ensure that you are meeting grade level expectations.

> The **sequence** of the content identifies in what order the content is taught. Knowing the order in which you should cover the material will help to ensure that you are meeting grade level expectations.

II. Choosing Content and Standards to Meet Grade Level Expectations

Step 1: Select Content and Standards

Begin your selection of content by looking at your state's standards for the grade level at which you will teach the lesson. For example, if you are teaching in Florida, you will visit the Florida Department of Education website for *Collaborate, Plan, Learn, Motivate, and Share (CPALMS): Standards* at http://www.cpalms.org/standards/flstandardsearch.aspx.

You will see that the standards are categorized by subject and grade level. Sometimes, multiple grade levels are covered in a standard. Skim through the standards to identify the one that fits the content you will teach.

Step 2: Review Content and Standards across Grade Levels

Once you select the content and standard, review the same content and related standards across grade levels. It's a good idea to look at the content and standards for the grade below yours and the grade after yours. When you do, you will be able to see the scope and sequence for the content and standards. Doing so will help you ensure that students meet grade level expectations, not those of the previous grade or next grade, unless you are making accommodations for diverse learners (e.g., remedial, gifted).

Example of Comparing and Contrasting Content and Standards

In this example, I have selected one standard at the elementary level and one at the secondary level so that those of you preparing to be teachers at these levels can connect to the information more readily.

In a science lesson, you may be teaching about the term or concept of gravity to your third grade class. The Florida standard for that content is listed below.

SC.3.E.5.4: Explore the Law of Gravity by demonstrating that gravity is a force that can be overcome.

Perhaps you may be teaching about gravity at the high school level. In that case, the following standard would guide your teaching.

SC.912.P.12.4: Describe how the gravitational force between two objects depends on their masses and the distance between them.

Comparing these two content standards shows you the scope, or depth, of the content. The depth of the content at grade three for the concept of gravity focuses on naming the force and demonstrating it. In high school, the mathematical formula of Newton's Law of Gravity is covered, which allows the students to understand the concept in much greater depth. The sequence of the content is also visible in this example, since first students must understand that there is a force called gravity and see what it does (grade three) before being able to understand how to calculate gravitational force (high school).

Step 3: Review Grade Level Textbooks and Materials

Additionally, you will find that the appropriate content is located in the grade level textbooks and accompanying materials purchased by your school. Publishing companies develop the texts to match the content, grade level expectations, and standards for each grade. In some cases, the publishing company develops texts specifically for a state, in which case the state standards will be located in the teacher's editions of the texts. Also within the teacher's edition, most publishing companies tend include a scope and sequence chart for the content taught in the textbook to assist teachers with their lesson planning.

Conclusion

Be sure that you understand the terms presented here; understanding the vocabulary of the field is essential to becoming a professional. To ensure that you are selecting appropriate content and standards for your lesson, follow the three-step process described here. In this way, you will ensure that your students meet grade level expectations.

Samples of Academic Content

Subject: Reading and Language Arts

Categories	Example Terms or Concepts
fiction	characterization, plot, theme
grammar	noun, pronoun, verb
vocabulary	context, definition, syllabification
writing	essay, paragraph, research paper

Subject: Mathematics

Categories	Example Terms or Concepts
algebra	coefficients, equations, exponents
basic operations	addition, multiplication, subtraction
geometry	angles, formulas for area, parallel
graphs	axis, linear, numerical data

Subject: Science

Categories	Example Terms or Concepts
biology	animals, cells, photosynthesis
chemistry	atom, Periodic Table, thermal
geology	glaciers, plate tectonics, volcanoes
physics	acceleration, kinetic energy, velocity

Subject: Social Studies

Categories	Example Terms or Concepts
geography	archipelago, compass rose, topographical map
history	American Revolution, slavery, voting
psychology	psychological disorders, self-esteem, stress
sociology	dominant ideology, genocide, norms

5.2

Activity 7: Identifying Content and Standards

Directions:

Review the information in this module and Module 3; then, complete the items below. Be sure to cite and reference your work. Remember to submit the final product to your instructor on the due date.

Item 1 – Selecting Content and Standards

1. List the grade level.
2. Name the subject.
3. State the content: the term or concept.
4. Identify the standard.

Item 2 – Comparing and Contrasting Content and Standards

1. Review the content and standard for the grade level below the one at which you will be teaching your lesson.
2. Identify the standard.
3. Examine the content and standard for the grade level above the one at which you will be teaching your lesson.
4. Identify the standard.

Note: If the content is not taught at the grade level above or below the one at which you will be teaching, indicate that such is the case.

Item 3 – Reviewing Textbooks and Materials

1. Provide the full reference for the textbook and accompanying materials that you will be using.
2. If you have access to the teacher's edition, identify if it contains your state's standards.
3. If you have access to the teacher's edition, identify if it contains a scope and sequence chart.

Note: If you don't have access to the teacher's edition, indicate that such is the case.

Module 5 References and Sources

Arends, R. I. (2012). *Learning to teach* (9th ed.). New York: McGraw-Hill.

Borich, G. D. (2014). *Effective teaching methods* (8th ed.). Upper Saddle River, NJ: Pearson.

Burden, P. R., & Byrd, D. M. (2013). *Methods for effective teaching: Meeting the needs of all students* (6th ed.). Upper Saddle River, NJ: Pearson.

Estes, T. H., Mintz, S. L., & Gunter, M. A., (2011). *Instruction: A models approach* (6th ed.) Upper Saddle River, NJ: Pearson.

Florida Department of Education (FL DOE). (2012). *Collaborate, plan, learn, motivate, and share (CPALMS): Standards.* Retrieved from http://www.cpalms.org/standards/flstandardsearch.aspx

Oliva, P. F., & Gordon, W. R., III. (2013). *Developing the curriculum* (8th ed.). Upper Saddle River, NJ: Pearson.

Module 6
Goals and Objectives

Critical Attributes of Goals and Objectives

Introduction

When writing a goal and related objectives, use the appropriate domain. The cognitive domain is used to help students develop intellectually. The affective domain is used to help students develop socially and emotionally. (Please note that standards for the affective domain are frequently listed under the area of Health.)

In order to write a good goal and related objectives, be sure that you attend to the following attributes.

Attribute 1
Make the goal and related objectives **grade appropriate** by ensuring that they reflect the grade level **state standard(s)** you selected to address in the lesson.

Attribute 2
Use the **same content** in the goal and related objectives (i.e., consistency in terms).

Attribute 3
Use the **appropriate level of the domain.** Make the goal at the highest level possible. Begin the related objectives at the lowest level, and work up to the highest level as stated in the goal.

Attribute 4
Use **specificity and clarity** by writing the goal and related objectives in precise and simple terms.

Attribute 5
Make the goal and related objectives **cohesive and complete.** The goal and each related objective should relate to the others and yet be able to stand alone.

Attribute 6
Use **correct grammar and spelling.**

Verbs for Writing Cognitive Goals and Objectives

Level 1: Remember

cite	know	match	recount	see	write
collect	label	memorize	relate	show	
compile	learn	name	repeat	specify	
define	list	read	record	state	
duplicate	listen	recall	remember	tell	
enumerate	locate	recite	say	view	

Level 2: Understand

choose	explain	identify	present	retell	translate
describe	express	itemize	recognize	review	understand
detect	find*	locate	report	select	verify*
discuss	gather	obtain	restate	show	

* as in locate

Level 3: Apply

act	display	illustrate	operate	repair	use
answer	dramatize	implement	perform	research	work
apply	employ	install	plan	search	
calculate	exhibit	interview	play	show	
check	experiment	make	portray	simulate	
complete	exemplify	manipulate	practice	solve	
demonstrate	graph	match	prepare	trace	

Level 4: Analyze

analyze	contrast	discover	explore	investigate	scrutinize
arrange	convert	distinguish	group	organize	search
categorize	detect	dissect	include	parse	simplify
choose	determine	divide	inquire	probe	study
classify	diagnose	establish	inspect	question	survey
compare*	diagram	estimate	interpret	reason	test
criticize	differentiate	examine	inventory	separate	uncover

* as in similarities and differences

Level 5: Evaluate

appraise	conceive	deduce	infer	propose	score
argue	conclude	defend	interpret	rate	summarize
assess	criticize	determine	judge	react to	support
characterize	critique	estimate	justify	recommend	value
choose	debate	evaluate	measure	revise	
compare*	decide	forecast	predict	select	

* for purposes of making a judgment or decision

Level 6: Create

adjust	compose	develop	imagine	predict	resolve
arrange	concoct	devise	incorporate	prepare	sequence
assemble	conduct	edit	invent	pretend	suppose
blend	construct	fabricate	make	produce	synthesize
brainstorm	contrive	formulate	modify	propose	systematize
build	convert	generalize	organize	prove	
change	create	generate	originate	rearrange	
combine	design	hypothesize	plan	relate	

Sample Cognitive Objectives

Introduction

When reviewing these samples of cognitive goals and objectives, see if you can identify their critical attributes as described in Module 6.1. Also, note that information is provided for further exploration of the content for each sample.

Sample #1

Standard
MA.5.A.6.2 Use the order of operations to simplify expressions which include exponents and parentheses.

Goal
The students can create an expression using exponents.

Objective 1
The students can record the results of integers raised to powers (i.e., exponents).

Objective 2
The students can explain how to solve an expression using exponents.

Objective 3
The students can demonstrate and illustrate the use of exponents in an expression.

Objective 4
The students can convert products using exponents written in standard form.

Objective 5
The students can predict answers to expressions using exponents.

Objective 6
The students can devise word problems using exponents.

For information about **expressions and exponents,** use the following website.

Stapel, E. (2013). *Purplemath. Simplifying expressions with exponents.* Retrieved from
http://www.purplemath.com/modules/simpexpo.htm

Sample #2

Standard
MA.3.A.1.1 Model multiplication and division including problems presented in context: repeated addition, multiplicative comparison, array, how many combinations, measurement, and partitioning.

Goal
The students can create word problems with multiplication and division.

Objective 1
The students can specify the correct operation (i.e., multiplication or division) for word problems.

Objective 2
The students can explain why an operation (i.e., multiplication or division) is used to solve word problems.

Objective 3
The students can solve word problems using the correct operation (i.e., multiplication or division).

Objective 4
The students can differentiate among the correct operations (i.e., multiplication or division) when solving word problems.

Objective 5
The students can predict which operation (i.e., multiplication or division) to use when solving word problems.

Objective 6
The students can formulate word problems using each operation (i.e., multiplication and division).

Use the website below to find sample **word problems**.

Youth Education Systems. (2011). *Thinking blocks. Multiplication and division word problems*. Retrieved from
http://www.thinkingblocks.com/thinkingblocks_md/tb_md_main.html

Sample #3

Standard
LA.8.3.4.4 The student will edit for correct use of the eight parts of speech (noun, pronoun, verb, adverb, adjective, conjunction, preposition, interjection), regular and irregular verbs, and pronoun agreement.

Goal
The students can produce sentences and paragraphs using the appropriate types of pronouns.

Objective 1
The students can know the definition and types of pronouns.

Objective 2
The students can identify pronouns and their type that are used in sentences and paragraphs.

Objective 3
The students can apply their knowledge of pronouns and type by using them correctly in sentences and paragraphs.

Objective 4
The students can parse sentences in a paragraph to choose and label the pronouns by type.

Objective 5
The students can appraise the use of pronouns and their types in sentences and paragraphs.

Objective 6
The students can incorporate pronouns by type into their own sentences and paragraphs.

Use the website below for information on the **types of pronouns**.

Grammar-Monster.com. (n.d.). *Types of pronouns.* Retrieved from
http://www.grammar-monster.com/lessons/pronouns_different_types.htm

Sample #4

Standard

LA.910.2.1.5: The student will analyze and develop an interpretation of a literary work by describing an author's use of literary elements (e.g., theme, point of view, characterization, setting, plot), and explain and analyze different elements of figurative language (e.g., simile, metaphor, personification, hyperbole, symbolism, allusion, imagery)

Goal

The students can synthesize a characterization of the protagonist and antagonist in the novel using descriptions of these characters' physical characteristics, communications, morals, and behaviors.

Objective 1

The students can read the novel, focusing on characterization of the protagonist and antagonist by locating their physical characteristics, communications, morals, and behaviors.

Subobjective 2

The students can discuss the novel, focusing on characterization of the protagonist and antagonist by describing their physical characteristics, communications, morals, and behaviors.

Subobjective 3

The students can portray characterizations of the protagonist and antagonist in the novel using examples of their physical characteristics, communications, morals, and behaviors.

Subobjective 4

The students can compare and contrast the physical characteristics, communications, morals, and behaviors of the protagonist and antagonist in the novel to examine their characterization.

Subobjective 5

The students can defend their characterizations of the protagonist and antagonist in the novel and how the protagonist's and antagonist's physical characteristics, communications, morals, and behaviors supported the characterization.

Subobjective 6

The students can propose different physical characteristics, communications, morals, and behaviors that might have changed the characterization of the protagonist and antagonist in the novel.

For information on **characterization in novels**, see the following website.

National Writing project. (n.d.). *Characterization in novels.* Retreived from http://digitalis.nwp.org/resource/3232

Note. The standards cited here are taken from the following source.
Florida Department of Education (FL DOE). (2012). *Collaborate, plan, learn, motivate, and share (CPALMS): Standards.* Retrieved from http://www.cpalms.org/standards/flstandardsearch.aspx

Phrases for Writing Affective Goals and Objectives

Level 1: Receiving

admit	comprehend	willing
attend	listen actively	
aware	recognize information	
become ready	take in information	

Level 2: Responding

applaud	describe behavior	question
assist	describe feelings	share
be courteous	demonstrate respect	show
check impressions	paraphrase	tell
communicate openly	partake	trust
demonstrate approval	participate	verify
demonstrate feelings	perform	
demonstrate how to	provide feedback	

Level 3: Valuing

appraise	join	recognize value
assess	judge worth	review critically
evaluate	justify	select
explain	propose	share
express appreciation	qualify	support
identify clearly	rate	value

Level 4: Organization

adhere to values	develop resolutions/ solutions	integrate solutions
alter behavior		modify behavior
arrange	find commonalities	resolve conflict(s)
balance	find connections	solve problem(s)
combine approaches	influence others	work out problem(s)
compare options	initiate behavior	

Level 5: Characterization

act	demonstrate consistently	distinguish consistently
behave responsibly	demonstrate predictably	individualize
behave consistently	display continuously	perform continuously

6.4

Sample Affective Objectives

Introduction

When reviewing these samples of affective goals and objectives, see if you can identify their critical attributes as described in Module 6.1. Also, note that information is provided for further exploration of the content for each sample.

Sample # 1

Standard
HE.K.B.4.1 Recognize healthy ways to express needs, wants, and feelings.

Goal
The students can consistently demonstrate their ability to express needs, wants, and feelings positively, rather than using their hands, feet, and objects in a negative way (e.g., hitting, kicking, or throwing things).

Objective 1
The students can comprehend why it is important to express their needs, wants, and feelings positively, rather than using their hands, feet, and objects in a negative way.

Objective 2
The students can demonstrate through role playing how to express their needs, wants, and feelings positively, rather than using their hands, feet, and objects in a negative way.

Objective 3
The students can express appreciation to their classmates who express their needs, wants, and feelings positively, rather than using their hands, feet, and objects in a negative way.

Objective 4
The students can develop and apply alternative solutions to problems that positively express their needs, wants, and feelings, rather than using their hands, feet, and objects in a negative way.

Objective 5
The students can consistently demonstrate their ability to positively express their needs, wants, and feelings, rather than using their hands, feet, and objects in a negative way.

To help students learn to manage anger, check out the following website.

Reach and Teach. (n.d.). *Hot stuff to help kids chill out: Anger management*. Retrieved from http://www.reachandteach.com/content/article.php/2009042713 1824839

Sample #2

Standard
HE.3.B.4.1 Identify effective verbal and nonverbal communication skills to enhance health.

Goal
The students can consistently demonstrate the effective verbal and nonverbal communication skill of active listening.

Objective 1
The students can recognize information about effective verbal and nonverbal communication skill that defines the attributes of active listening.

Objective 2
The students can demonstrate the effective verbal and nonverbal communication skill of listening actively when together in class.

Objective 3
The students can express appreciation to those who use the effective verbal and nonverbal communication skill of listening actively.

Objective 4
The students can resolve conflicts that arise by using the effective verbal and nonverbal communication skill of listening actively.

Objective 5
The students can consistently demonstrate the effective verbal and nonverbal communication skill of listening actively in all areas of the school.

For activities related to active listening, visit the following website.

Electronic Resource Center for human Rights Education. (n.d.). *Opening the door to nonviolence. Part 1, Workshop 2: Skills for active listening.* Retrieved from http://www.hrea.org/erc/Library/primary/Opening_the_Door/workshop2.html

---

Sample #3

Standard
HE.7.P.7.2 Experiment with behaviors that will maintain or improve personal health and reduce health risks.

Goal
The students can continuously display respect for others in order to develop healthy relationship skills.

Objective 1
The students can comprehend information presented on the attributes of the skill of displaying respect in order to develop healthy relationship skills.

Objective 2
The students can participate in activities that demonstrate the skill of displaying respect in order to develop healthy relationship skills.

Objective 3
The students can value demonstrations of respect within class in order to develop healthy relationship skills.

Objective 4
The students can influence others to display respect within class in order to develop healthy relationship skills.

Objective 5
The students can continuously display respect for others within school in order to develop healthy relationship skills.

For more information on development of respect and other character traits, visit the following website.

Josephson Institute Center for Youth Studies. (2013). *Character counts.* Retrieved from http://charactercounts.org/

Note: The standards cited here are taken from the following source.
Florida Department of Education (FL DOE). (2012). *Collaborate, plan, learn, motivate, and share (CPALMS): Standards.* Retrieved from http://www.cpalms.org/standards/flstandardsearch.aspx

Activity 8: Writing a Cognitive Goal and Objectives

Directions:

This activity provides you with an opportunity to receive feedback on your lesson plan goal and objectives. **Review** the information in this module; then, complete the items below. Remember to **submit** the final product to your instructor on the due date.

1. Start with the **standard** you will be addressing.
2. Next, for the **goal**, remember to use a verb at the highest domain level (i.e., create).
3. For the first **objective**, use a verb at the lowest level (i.e., remember) and continue to the next highest level as you write each objective.
4. Check to make sure that your goal and objectives meet all the **critical attributes** of goals and objectives.
5. **Review and edit** your assignment for clarity, accuracy, grammar, and mechanics.
6. Be sure to **cite and reference** your work.

Standard

Goal

Objective 1

Objective 2

Objective 3

Objective 4

Objective 5

Objective 6

Activity 9: Writing an Affective Goal and Objectives

Directions:

This activity provides you with an opportunity to receive feedback on your lesson plan goal and objectives. **Review** the information in this module; then, complete the items below. Remember to **submit** the final product to your instructor on the due date.

1. Start with the **standard** you will be addressing.
2. Next, for the **goal**, remember to use a verb at the highest domain level (i.e., characterization).
3. For the first **objective**, use a verb at the lowest level (i.e., receiving) and continue to the next highest level as you write each objective.
4. Check to make sure that your goal and objectives meet all the **critical attributes** of goals and objectives.
5. **Review and edit** your assignment for clarity, accuracy, grammar, and mechanics.
6. Be sure to **cite and reference** your work.

Standard

Goal

Objective 1

Objective 2

Objective 3

Objective 4

Objective 5

Module 6 References and Sources

Anderson, L. W., Krathwohl, D. R., Airasian, P. W., Cruikshank, K. A., Mayer, R. E., Pintrich, P. R., Raths, J., & Wittrock, M. C. (2001). *A taxonomy for learning, teaching, and assessing: a revision of Bloom's taxonomy of educational objectives*. New York: Longman.

Arends, R. I. (2012). *Learning to teach* (9th ed.). New York: McGraw-Hill.

Borich, G. D. (2014). *Effective teaching methods* (8th ed.). Upper Saddle River, NJ: Pearson.

Burden, P. R., & Byrd, D. M. (2013). *Methods for effective teaching: Meeting the needs of all students* (6th ed.). Boston: Allyn & Bacon.

Electronic Resource Center for human Rights Education. (n.d.). *Opening the door to nonviolence. Part 1, Workshop 2: Skills for active listening.* Retrieved from http://www.hrea.org/erc/Library/primary/Opening_the_Door/workshop2.html

Engine-Uity, Ltd. (1984). *Verbs and products for independent study.* Phoenix, AZ: Engine-Uity, Ltd.

Estes, T. H., Mintz, S. L., & Gunter, M. A., (2011). *Instruction: A models approach* (6th ed.) Upper Saddle River, NJ: Pearson.

Florida Department of Education (FL DOE). (2012). *Collaborate, plan, learn, motivate, and share (CPALMS): Standards.* Retrieved from http://www.cpalms.org/standards/flstandardsearch.aspx

Grammar-Monster.com. (n.d.). *Types of pronouns.* Retrieved from http://www.grammar-monster.com/lessons/pronouns_different_types.htm

Gray, M. B., Nelson, A., & Gorman, D. A. (1988). *Planning content and goals* (Learning Package 1). Florida Coalition for the Development of a Performance Measurement System. Tallahassee, FL: State Department of Education.

Gronlund, N. (1970). *Stating behavioral objectives for classroom instruction.* New York: Macmillan.

Josephson Institute Center for Youth Studies. (2013). *Character counts.* Retrieved from http://charactercounts.org/

Krathwohl, D. R., Bloom, B. S., & Masia, B. B. (1964). *Taxonomy of educational objectives, Handbook II: Affective domain.* New York: Longman.

Mager, R. F. (1997). *Preparing instructional objectives: A critical tool in the development of effective instruction.* Los Angeles: Center for Effective Instruction.

National Writing project. (n.d.). *Characterization in novels.* Retrieved from http://digitalis.nwp.org/resource/3232

Reach and Teach. (n.d.). *Hot stuff to help kids chill out: Anger management.* Retrieved from http://www.reachandteach.com/content/article.php/20090427131824839

Stapel, E. (2013). *Purplemath. Simplifying expressions with exponents.* Retrieved from http://www.purplemath.com/modules/simpexpo.htm

Victor, B., & Kellough, R. D. (2000). *Science for the elementary and middle school* (9th ed.). Upper Saddle River, NJ: Merrill.

Youth Education Systems. (2011). *Thinking blocks: Multiplication and division word problems.* Retrieved from http://www.thinkingblocks.com/thinkingblocks_md/tb_md_main.html

6.8

Module 7
Learning Accommodations for Special Populations

Defining Special Populations

The term special population refers to any classification of students who need specific accommodations in order to learn successfully. These special populations include, but are not limited to, the following students: English Speakers of Other Languages (ESOL), Exceptional Student Education (ESE), Drop Out Prevention (DOP), Economically Disadvantaged or Remedial (i.e., Title 1), and Gifted.

Courtesy of Fotolia

As a teacher, you are required by federal and state laws to address the needs of these special populations, since all students are entitled to an education in the regular classroom. As a result, you must modify lessons to accommodate these diverse learners' needs to insure their success. Holding the belief that all children can learn begins that process! Also, in some schools, there are special programs and practitioners available to assist special population students and you. The most common program options are defined here.

ESOL Programs are designed to assist students whose first language isn't English to acquire English language skills. Students are assessed and classified according to their level of English proficiency and receive instructional services commensurate with their classification. Once students achieve the highest classification, they are released from services. ESOL specialists and regular classroom teachers are mandated to accommodate ESOL students so that they can be successful at learning.

ESE Programs provide services to students who are diagnosed with a disability. A student's disability is diagnosed through an evaluation that includes data collected from multiple sources, and an individualized educational plan (IEP) is designed to meet the disabled student's learning needs. Exceptional education and regular classroom teachers are mandated to follow the IEP in order to help the student meet the learning objectives designed for him/her.

Remedial Programs are typically referred to as Title 1 Programs. In these remedial programs students receive instruction designed to help them improve their basic skills, usually in reading and mathematics. Remedial and regular classroom teachers work together to help the students be successful in their learning.

Drop Out Prevention Programs may begin as early as the fourth grade, when students who are at-risk of dropping out of school may be identified. These programs provide a variety of experiences that assist DOP students with development of academic and social skills needed to be successful at learning.

Enrichment programs are used mainly with gifted students but also have been found to be effective with at-risk students such as DOP. Enrichment programs are designed to provide students with opportunities to develop problem solving and research skills, engage their creativity, allow them to explore knowledge at a greater depth than minimum standards, and motivate them to excel.

Teacher Behaviors that Demonstrate Acceptance of Special Populations

Courtesy of Fotolia

Develop a caring climate.
- ✓ Be trustworthy; do what you say you will do.
- ✓ Accept students' differences.
- ✓ Expect that all students can learn.
- ✓ Praise academic success and encourage good behavior.

Employ teaching and learning accommodations.
- ✓ Teach using diverse methods that address students' learning styles.
- ✓ Encourage students to think and ask questions. No question is ever stupid; it shows that students are thinking.
- ✓ Provide students enough wait time to think and respond to a question or problem.
- ✓ Offer alternative ways for your students to respond to a question or problem.
- ✓ Provide ample opportunities for practice of newly learned content.
- ✓ Give specific feedback to students on their academics and behavior.
- ✓ Use alternative ways to monitor and assess learning.

Provide a well-organized classroom.
- ✓ Use strategic seating for students in order to avoid discrimination and enhance participation.
- ✓ Provide opportunities for students to work with buddies and/or in small groups.
- ✓ Post rules, consequences, schedules, etc. in clear and concise language and use graphics.

Tips for Modifying Lesson Plans for Special Populations

Courtesy of Fotolia

Introduction
These pages contain suggestions that will help you accommodate your special population students' learning needs. The boxes align with the sections of the lesson plan presented in Module 1.

Context
Consider the context—the special populations in your class—as you develop your lesson plan. Remember to incorporate students' cultural and world views.

Instructional Materials
When selecting the materials for your lesson, be sure to include items that address the learning needs of your special population students. For example, use graphic organizers, manipulatives, "adapted" reading passages, etc. Use a variety of materials to address students' learning styles.

Set
When you select your motivational tools, pay particular attention to choosing things that will interest your special population students while accommodating their learning needs (e.g., using large font on an advance organizer for a visually impaired student). Connecting to experiences is one way to motivate students and incorporate their cultural and world views.

Content, Grade Level Expectations, and Standards
Identify the content and standard for your lesson, being sure to review what is covered in the grade levels below and above the grade level at which you will teach. Use the content and standards from these different grade levels to modify what you teach based on the needs of your special population students (e.g., remedial or gifted).

Goals and Objectives
Write the goals and objectives for your lesson adding any additional information that you will need to insure that your special population students are accommodated. For example, ESE students may have different objectives as per their individualized educational plans.

Accommodations

Identify the content-based vocabulary and teach it before teaching the content of the lesson. Provide specific instruction for the vocabulary using easily understood synonyms in the definitions and graphics when applicable. Identify the parts of speech to promote learning of English grammar. Consider having your students keep vocabulary note books where all new content-based vocabulary and definitions are listed for review and study.

Instruction

Use a variety of instructional strategies (e.g., Think-Pair-Share, small group work) so that all learners are accommodated. Display teacher behaviors that call attention to important material (e.g., marker expressions). Pace your lesson so that all students can successfully complete it, providing extended time for those who need it. Modify student activities as needed to meet special population students' learning needs. For example, some students may need to complete fewer problems on a math worksheet. Other students may need extended time to finish independent reading tasks.

Classroom Management

Use strategic seating to accommodate those students who need it. Maintain student interest to avoid potential behavior problems that occur from students drifting off task. For example, you may help a student with ADHD maintain interest by using reward tokens when the student has attended to the task at hand for specific time intervals.

Monitoring and Assessment

Identify what will be done to effectively monitor and assess special population students. For example, to monitor ESOL students' understanding of the material as you are teaching, you may want to have these students give you a special signal (e.g., raise their pinky finger) when they don't understand something so that you can help them. When assessing special population students, the assessments themselves may need to be modified. For example, a learning disabled student may need to answer reading questions orally as opposed to on paper.

Closure

In order to accommodate special population students, be sure to close the lesson with a complete review of the material covered in order to reinforce learning.

Activity 10: Selecting Instructional Strategies for Special Populations

Directions:

There are literally hundreds of instructional strategies that are used to accommodate the needs of special populations. In this activity you will learn more about these strategies by conducting a web quest. First, review the information in this module; then, complete the items below. Remember to submit the final product to your instructor on the due date.

1. Start your web quest with the links provided below, but you are welcome to find your own web sites as well.

2. Remember to consider the special populations in your field experiences classroom as you complete the web quest.

3. Select three to five strategies for use in your lesson plan assignment.

4. Name the strategies and describe how you will use them to accommodate students with special populations in your lesson.

5. Be sure to cite and reference your work.

Some Suggested Websites

About.com Special Education. (2013). *Instructional strategies and lesson plans for special educators.* Retrieved from
http://specialed.about.com/od/teacherstrategies/Teaching_Strategies_and_Best_Practices.htm

Broward County Public Schools Multicultural, ESOL and Program Services Department. (2012). *Strategies for ELLs.* Retrieved from
http://www.broward.k12.fl.us/esol/Eng/BestPractices/index.html

National Association for Gifted Children. (2008). *What the research says: Gifted education works.* Retrieved from
http://www.nagc.org/giftededucationworks.aspx

National Drop Out Prevention Center/Network. (2013). *Effective strategies for dropout prevention.* Retrieved from
http://www.dropoutprevention.org/effective-strategies

Osceola County School District. (2007). *ESOL strategies chart.* Retrieved from
http://www.osceola.k12.fl.us/depts/Multicultural_Education_Department/documents/ESOLStrategieswithdefinitions.pdf

Rowan, K. J. (2010). *Glossary of instructional strategies.* Retrieved from
http://www.beesburg.com/edtools/glossary.html

Module 7 References and Sources

About.com Special Education. (2013). *Instructional strategies and lesson plans for special educators.* Retrieved from http://specialed.about.com/od/teacherstrategies/Teaching_Strategies_and_Best_Practices.htm

Arends, R. I. (2012). *Learning to teach* (9th ed.). New York: McGraw-Hill.

Borich, G. D. (2014). *Effective teaching methods* (8th ed.). Upper Saddle River, NJ: Pearson.

Broward County Public Schools Multicultural, ESOL and Program Services Department. (2012). *Strategies for ELLs.* Retrieved from http://www.broward.k12.fl.us/esol/Eng/BestPractices/index.html

Burden, P. R., & Byrd, D. M. (2013). *Methods for effective teaching: Meeting the needs of all students* (6th ed.). Boston: Allyn & Bacon.

Estes, T. H., Mintz, S. L., & Gunter, M. A., (2011). *Instruction: A models approach* (6th ed.) Upper Saddle River, NJ: Pearson.

Florida Department of Education (1999). *Language arts through ESOL: A guide for teachers and administrators.* A companion to the Sunshine State Standards for language arts.

Gifted and talented education. (2013). Retrieved from http://www.answers.com/topic/gifted-and-talented-education

Learning Disabilities Council. (1991). *Glossary of Learning Disabilities Terms.* Richmond, VA: Author. Retrieved from http://www.ldonline.org/ld_indepth/glossaries/ld_glossary.html

National Association for Gifted Children. (2008). *What the research says: Gifted education works.* Retrieved from http://www.nagc.org/giftededucationworks.aspx

National Drop Out Prevention Center/Network. (2013). *Effective strategies for dropout prevention.* Retrieved from http://www.dropoutprevention.org/effective-strategies

Osceola County School District. (2007). *ESOL strategies chart.* Retrieved from http://www.osceola.k12.fl.us/depts/Multicultural_Education_Department/documents/ESOLStrategieswithdefinitions.pdf

Rowan, K. J. (2010). *Glossary of instructional strategies.* Retrieved from http://www.beesburg.com/edtools/glossary.html

Tulare, N. B. (1998). *Teaching tips for the ESOL classroom.* Retrieved from http://www.nwlink.com/~tulare/tchngtips.html

Module 8
Instruction

Module 8.1
Methods, Strategies, and Models

Teaching Methods, Strategies, and Models Defined

Courtesy of Fotolia

Method

A method is a **step-by-step procedure** for teaching your subject or content. You select the method based on the subject, content, and which type of knowledge you will teach.

Strategy

A strategy is a **tool** that is a part of a method or enhances the method (e.g., advance organizer, extending thinking).

Model

- A model is a method or step-by-step procedure that you use to teach which **requires specific strategies for each step in the procedure**.
- The six most frequently used teaching models are presentation, concept teaching, direct instruction, cooperative learning, problem-based instruction, and discussion.
- Presentation, concept teaching, and direct instruction are **teacher-centered** models in that the teacher controls the teaching-learning process. Cooperative learning, problem-based instruction, and discussion are **student-centered** models in that the teacher becomes a facilitator, and the students have more voice in how learning occurs.
- To help choose the correct teaching model for the subject and content you want to teach, identify what type of knowledge it is. **Factual knowledge** is information that is a fact; it can be proven as true and is not an opinion. **Conceptual knowledge** is an idea; facts can be grouped together to generate a concept. **Procedural knowledge** is information that tells how to do something. **Metacognitive knowledge** refers to thinking about the big picture—multiple types of knowledge and knowing when to apply them. Please review the information on Study Skills in Module 1.5 and the rest of this module for examples of the types of knowledge.

Examples of Teaching Strategies

Introduction

The following lists of teaching strategies are organized around the parts of the lesson plan in which they are used. The list isn't meant to be all inclusive, but it should spark your thinking about the teaching-learning process! Please consider incorporating some of these strategies in the appropriate sections of your lesson plan.

Set
- State the **goal** of the lesson.
- Pose a **question**.
- Present an **advance organizer**—auditorally or visually.
- Show a short **video or video clip**.
- Present a **graphic organizer**.
- Share a **personal experience**—yours and/or the students.

Instruction
- Define **content-based vocabulary**.
- Present **information**.
- Offer **examples and non-examples** of terms or concepts.
- Give a **demonstration**.
- Provide **guided practice**.
- Facilitate **cooperative learning groups**.
- Assist **independent and group investigations**.
- Model an **experiment**.
- Explain **procedures**.
- Model a **behavior**.
- Hold, focus, and end a **discussion**.
- Pace varied **activities**.
- Assign **homework for extended practice**.
- Employ **family involvement activities**.

Monitoring and Assessment

- Use **recitation** to check for understanding.
- Provide **feedback—positive and constructive**.
- **Correct** assignments.
- Review the **advance organizer**.
- **Test** for attainment.
- Employ **student presentations**.
- Use **alternative assessments**.

Closure

- **Review** the content.
- **Summarize** the content.
- Discuss students' **thinking processes**.
- **Debrief** the discussion.
- Discuss students' **problem solving processes**.

Note. See Module 11 for tips on how to close a lesson.

Room Arrangements for Various Teaching Models

Introduction

Different teaching methods, strategies, and models require different room arrangements. Consider the following options.

Teacher-centered Models

When using the teaching models of presentation, concept teaching, and direct instruction, place the instructional area directly in front of the students. You will deliver the lesson from this vantage point, but you will need to move around the room too in order to monitor students' behavior and learning.

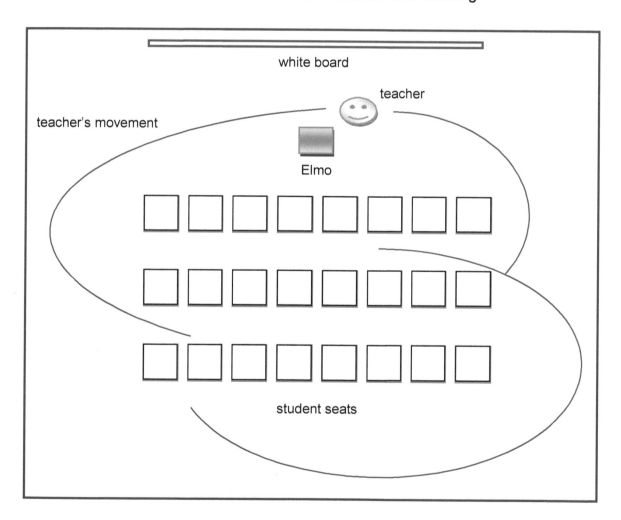

Student-centered Models

When using the teaching models of cooperative learning, problem-based instruction, and discussion, students typically sit in a group. Swing seating, "U" shape, or circular shape may also be used. As students work, you will need to move around the room in order to assist with group work and monitor students' behavior and learning.

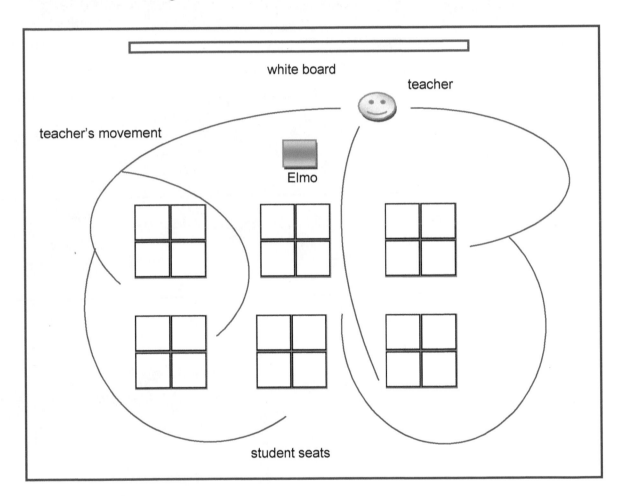

Activity 11: Identifying Appropriate Teaching Models

Directions:

Review the information in this module; then, complete the eight items in the table. Remember to submit the final product to your instructor on the due date.

1. Identify the type of knowledge for the content (i.e., factual, conceptual, procedural, etc.).

2. Select an appropriate teaching model for teaching that type of knowledge.

3. Provide a rationale for your selected teaching model. Consider the criteria in the following questions when providing your rationales.

    A. Does the model support learning of the standards, goals, and objectives that would be associated with the content?

    B. Will the model catch your students' attention and maintain motivation?

    C. Will the model provide opportunities for a variety of activities in the lesson that will help you address your students' learning styles and accommodate the needs of special populations?

    Note: You may use the back pages of the activity to write the rationales if you don't have enough room in the boxes. Or, you may type up the rationales as a Microsoft Word file, print the page, and attach it to the activity.

4. Review and edit your assignment for clarity, accuracy, grammar, and mechanics.

5. Remember to cite and reference your work.

Subject	Content	Type of Knowledge	Model	Rationale for Model Selection
Language Arts	Vocabulary			
Language Arts	Plot of a novel			
Math	Multiplication of fractions			
Math	Simplification of expressions with exponents			
Science	Experiment with precipitates			
Science	Photosynthesis			
Social Studies	Revolutionary War facts			
Social Studies	Genocide			

Module 8.2
Presentation

Tips to Extend Students' Thinking

Courtesy of Fotolia

> **Extending thinking** refers to strategies that you employ to promote students' thinking at a higher cognitive level than simple factual information.

Introduction

Review the information in Module 1.5 on Study Skills and Module 4 on Motivating Students. Then, take a look at the four tips recommended here to extend students' thinking at the end of a lesson.

Tip 1
Use a content analysis or concept map.
- Have students create a content analysis or concept map based on the facts discussed in the lesson. They will need to generate the concepts and/or generalizations.
- Give the students an incomplete content analysis or concept map. Consider having the students create the generalizations for the content analysis at the end of the lesson. Or, have the students label the relationships among the concepts in the concept map.

Tip 2
Return to the advance organizer.
- At the beginning of the lesson, present an advance organizer and pose a question that focuses students on categorizing the information that you will be presenting. Have the students take notes on the organizer during the lesson. At the end of the lesson, ask students to share how they answered the question you posed.

Tip 3

Discuss the graphic organizer.

- Ask students to summarize the information from the graphic organizer, having them focus on the big ideas or concepts.

Tip 4

Ask questions.

- Module 8.7 presents information on questioning strategies. Employ these strategies to extend students' thinking.

Activity 12: Selecting Strategies to Extend Thinking

Directions:

Review the information in this module, Module 1.5 on Study Skills, and Module 4 on Motivating Students. Then, complete the items below. Remember to submit the final product to your instructor on the due date.

Strategies to Extend Thinking

1. List the grade level.

2. Name the subject.

3. State the content: the term or concept.

4. Name a strategy that you will use to extend students' thinking.

5. Describe how you will use the selected strategy.

6. Explain how the strategy promotes students' thinking to a higher cognitive level than Levels 1 and 2 of the cognitive domain.

7. Review and edit your assignment for clarity, accuracy, grammar, and mechanics.

8. Remember to cite and reference your work.

Module 8.3
Concept Teaching

Defining Conceptual Information

Introduction

The content in academic disciplines is classified into **organizational systems**. These organizational systems make learning large amounts of information easier. For example, in science, animals are organized using the Linnaean Taxonomic System: kingdom, phylum, class, order, family, genus, and species. Whatever the discipline or classification system used for the conceptual information you will teach, describing the information clearly is essential.

To enhance **clarity**, you first will need to determine what conceptual information is **appropriate for the grade level** that you are teaching. Checking the grade level standards and textbooks will help with this task. Also, you may want to search on the internet for instructional materials that help define the conceptual information. However, when viewing these materials, keep in mind that the scope and sequence of the information becomes more complex as grade levels increase.

The four step process that follows will help you compose a **clear definition** of a term or concept that you will be teaching. Each of the steps contains an example. Notice that because the examples are at the third grade level, the term or concept is defined using simple language. The Linnaean Taxonomic System has been simplified as well (i.e., The category is identified as vertebrates in the animal kingdom, and the concept is mammals.). If this same term or concept was being taught in grade nine, you would use the Linnaean Taxonomic System as follows: the kingdom—animal, the phylum—vertebrates, and the class—mammals. So, you would actually use two categories and name them using the taxonomy.

Following the four-step process, you will find a graphic organizer that illustrates the example provided for each step in the process. Consider making an organizer such as the sample to further assist your students' learning.

Step 1 Delineate the term or concept.
- Name the term and define it using **synonyms** or short phrases that do NOT include the word being defined.

e.g., The term is mammals. The definition is animals that are warm-blooded; have hair; nurse their young; and have well developed brains, ears, and hearts.

Step 2 Identify the category or group.
- Name the category to which the concept belongs.

e.g., vertebrates in the animal kingdom

Step 3 Name the attributes.
- Define the **critical attributes**, which are the essential or required parts that make the term or concept what it is.

e.g., warm-blooded; have hair; nurse their young; and have well developed brains, ears, and hearts

- Define some **noncritical attributes**, which are nonessential parts that are not required to make the term or concept what it is.

e.g., where mammals live, what colors they are, and their sizes

Step 4 Provide Examples.
- Give **diverse examples** of the concept. The examples of the concept, of course, are from the <u>same category</u> and contain the <u>critical attributes</u>. However, the examples must also be <u>diverse in noncritical attributes</u>. Diverse examples prevent misunderstanding of the concept.

e.g., pig, dolphin, buffalo, and leopard

- Give **diverse non-examples** by using <u>different terms or concepts</u> from the <u>same category</u>.

e.g., parrot, turtle, fish, and butterfly

Graphic Organizer: Defining Mammals

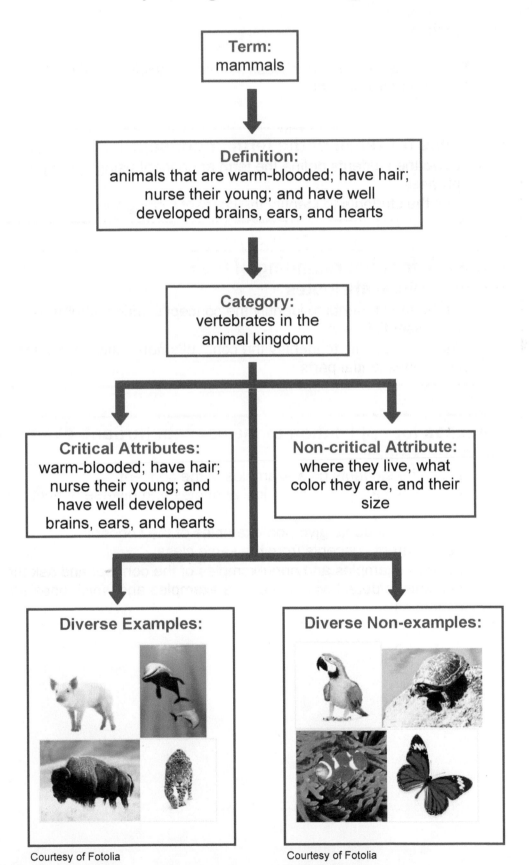

Term:
mammals

Definition:
animals that are warm-blooded; have hair; nurse their young; and have well developed brains, ears, and hearts

Category:
vertebrates in the animal kingdom

Critical Attributes:
warm-blooded; have hair; nurse their young; and have well developed brains, ears, and hearts

Non-critical Attribute:
where they live, what color they are, and their size

Diverse Examples:

Courtesy of Fotolia

Diverse Non-examples:

Courtesy of Fotolia

Assessing Students' Conceptual Knowledge

Introduction

Try these techniques to assess students' knowledge of the term or concept that you have taught.

---

1. Assess for recall of the term or concept and category.
- Have the students define the term or concept using synonyms or short phrases.
- Ask the students to identify the concept's category.

---

2. Assess for understanding of the term or concept's critical and noncritical attributes.
- Probe the students to identify the concept's critical attributes.
  i.e., essential parts
- Ask the students to identify the concept's non-critical attributes.
  i.e., nonessential parts

---

3. Assess for application of the concept through examples and non-examples.
- Have the students give examples of the concept.
  i.e., same category with critical attributes and diverse noncritical attributes
- Have the students give non-examples of the concept.
  i.e., different concepts from the same class
- Provide examples and non-examples of the concept and ask the students to detect which ones are examples and which ones are non-examples.

Activity 13: Practice Defining Conceptual Information

Directions:

Review the material from this module before starting this activity. Notice that the six items in the activity present definitions of terms or **concepts**. Each part of the definition has been lettered. In the spaces below each definition, identify whether the lettered part is the term or **concept name, category, or critical attributes**. Remember to **submit** the final product to your instructor on the due date.

---

1. **Repartee** is **a reply** that is **quick and witty**.
       A   B   C

   A. _____

   B. _____

   C. _____

---

2. The **part of a lock** that is **shot from and drawn back into the case by**
             A   B
   the action of the key is called **the bolt**.
                          C

   A. _____

   B. _____

   C. _____

---

3. **An animal** that **eats both plant and animal substances** is called **an**
        A   B
   omnivore.
     C

   A. _____

   B. _____

   C. _____

4. <u>Muscular dystrophy</u> is <u>a disease</u> which is <u>chronic and</u>
          A   B   C
<u>noncontagious</u>. It is of <u>unknown origin</u> and is <u>gradual in nature</u>, but
                      D   E
<u>leads to complete and irreversible muscular deterioration</u>.
              F

A. _____

B. _____

C. _____

D. _____

E. _____

F. _____

5. <u>A caption</u> that <u>explains symbols and the scale used on a map</u> is
     A   B
called <u>a map legend</u>.
         C

A. _____

B. _____

C. _____

6. <u>An out</u> is a play <u>in baseball or softball</u> in which there are <u>three strikes</u>
    A   B

   <u>against a batter</u>, <u>a ball is caught by a defensive player before it</u>
    C   D

   <u>touches the ground</u>, <u>a base runner is caught off base by a defensive</u>
                                               E

   <u>player who has the ball</u>, or <u>a defensive player who has the ball</u>
                                                     F

   <u>touches base before the runner arrives</u>.

A. _____

B. _____

C. _____

D. _____

E. _____

F. _____

Note: This activity is adapted from Collins, D. W., Purdom, D. M., & Fardig, G. E. (1985). *Teaching concepts. Activity 3.* Tallahassee, FL: Florida State Department of Education.

8.3.3

147

Activity 14: Practicing Selecting Examples and Non-examples of Conceptual Information

Directions:

Review the material in this module before beginning the activity. Start the activity by reading the items thoroughly, noting the **category** and term or **concept**. For each of the items given, select the **best set of examples and non-examples** for the term or concept. Place an "X" on the line in front of your selection. On the lines that follow the sets of examples and non-examples, give the **reason** why you chose your answer. Remember to **submit** the final product to your instructor on the due date.

---

1. **Category:** Vertebrates
   Term: Mammal

   Examples:
   _____ A. dog, horse, cat, pig
   _____ B. whale, bat, kangaroo, dog
   _____ C. lion, tiger, panther, cougar

   Reason: _____

   _____

   Non-examples:
   _____ A. trout, rattlesnake, woodpecker
   _____ B. rattlesnake, cobra, lizard
   _____ C. perch, bass, shark

   Reason: _____

   _____

---

2. **Category:** Inappropriate Behavior
   Term: Illegal Behavior

   Examples:
   _____ A. burglary, armed robbery, and shoplifting
   _____ B. speeding, reckless driving, and failure to yield right of way
   _____ C. burglary, speeding, and counterfeiting

   Reason: _____

   _____

   Non-examples:
   _____ A. cheating on tests, absenteeism, and rudeness
   _____ B. voting, military service, and jury duty
   _____ C. kindness, friendliness, and compassion

   Reason: _____

   _____

3. **Category:** Closed Geometric Shapes
   Term: Triangles

   Examples:

   _____ A.

   _____ B.

   _____ C.

   Reason: _____

   _____

   Non-examples:

   _____ A.

   _____ B.

   _____ C.

   Reason: _____

   _____

Note: This activity is adapted from Collins, D. W., Purdom, D. M., & Fardig, G. E. (1985). *Teaching concepts. Activity 5.* Tallahassee, FL: Florida State Department of Education.

Module 8.4
Direct Instruction

Task Analysis

Courtesy of Fotolia

❖ The term **task analysis** means to dissect complex skills, behaviors, or concepts into smaller and easier parts that can be better explained and taught.

❖ A task analysis . . .
- is based on the behaviorist philosophy,
- is used when learning a new skill,
- is used with students who cannot master complex tasks (e.g., children with autism, with mental illness, or young children), and
- enables identification of learning problems.

Steps for Analyzing and Teaching a Task

Step 1
Planning: Identify the task.
- Answer the question: How is this task done?
- Imagine the task and note individual subtasks.
- Perform the task and write down the individual subtasks.
- Watch a video or someone else perform the task and note individual subtasks.

Step 2
Planning: Break the task down into subtasks.
A. Specify objectives to be reached at the end of each subtask.
B. Determine the detail and number of subtasks based on your students' needs.
   e.g., The number of subtasks can range from a simple 3-5 to 20 or more subtasks.
C. Start with the smallest number of subtasks possible.
D. Chain or sequence the subtasks.

Step 3

Planning: Assess the effectiveness of your task analysis.
A. What is the scope of a task analysis?
B. How difficult are individual steps?
C. What are the beginning and the end of the task analysis?
D. Does the task analysis help with the transfer of knowledge?

Step 4

Instruction: Demonstrate the subtask to your students as you complete the task.
- Explain each subtask in the chain as you demonstrate it.

Step 5

Instruction: Guide the students as they complete the subtasks in the chain, providing feedback on accuracy.
Use the chain that is most appropriate for your students.
- Forward chain – Students start with the first subtask and work until reaching the end of the chain, completing the task.
- Backward chain – Students start by learning to perform the last subtask and continue learning subtasks from the end towards the beginning of the task, completing the task.
- Mixed chain – Students perform some of the subtasks, which can be the most difficult or the easiest subtask, adding new ones as they become proficient in each of them until they complete the task.

Step 6

Instruction: Assign extended practice.
- Give additional practice, continuing to provide feedback, until the task is mastered.

8.4.1

Homework

Introduction

These pages will help you to learn the following: the purposes of homework, how much homework is reasonable, the challenges that may arise with homework, tips for how you can make homework successful, and tips for how parents can make homework successful.

Purposes of Homework

Courtesy of Fotolia

- Fostering **learning**
- Enabling **practice** to enhance **retention and generalization**
- Providing opportunities to **revise and improve** work
- Evaluating **understanding** of content
- Encouraging **critical and creative thinking**
- Developing and practicing **study skills** and **moral character** (e.g., responsibility, independence)
- Sparking interest in **future learning**
- Stimulating the use of various **learning resources** (e.g., libraries, internet, etc.)

Amount of Homework

- Assign a **reasonable amount of homework** (i.e., not excessive and doesn't create a burden).
- **Coordinate with other teachers** at the grade level to ensure that the total amount of homework for students is reasonable.
- **Avoid** assigning homework on weekends, holidays, and vacations.
- Follow these **guidelines** for assigning homework each school day.
  Grades K-2 = 10-20 minutes
  Grades 3-5 = 30-60 minutes
  Grades 6-8 = 60-120 minutes
  Grades 9-12 = 60-180 minutes

Consider Homework Challenges

- Students' motivation
- Family environment (e.g., lack of supervision, time, and/or studying space; parents' limited education; etc.)
- Socioeconomic gaps among students (e.g., different access to learning resources)
- Students' personal issues (e.g., lack of good role models, drug or alcohol use, teenage pregnancy, etc.)

Tips for Teachers

Tip 1
- Insure that assignments reinforce the content taught or spark interest in new content.

e.g., practice in finding the area of a square after having a lesson on the same (reinforcement); students write down what they know about volcanoes before starting a lesson on the topic (spark interest)

Tip 2
- Set expectations for homework at the beginning of the school year.
- Share those expectations with students and parents.

e.g., 20 minutes of homework per school night, no homework on weekends and holidays; homework is checked for completion at the beginning of class; homework is collected for grading at the end of the class

Tip 3
- Always provide feedback on the assignment, and explain how the homework will be checked/graded.

e.g., self-checked in class, scored for a grade by the teacher, peer feedback, etc.

Tip 4
- Clearly describe the purpose of the homework and its connection to the lesson.

e.g., practice on two-digit division for better understanding and improved skill at performing the process

8.4.2

Tip 5

- Give specific directions for the homework and provide an example of how to complete the assignment.

e.g.,

Directions:

Underline the nouns in the sentences, and above the noun label whether it is *common* or *proper*.

Example:

        common   *common*   *common*

European <u>colonization</u> had multiple <u>effects</u> on the Native American <u>tribes</u>

   proper

of <u>Florida</u>.

Tip 6

- Give assignments that promote critical and creative thinking.

e.g., compare and contrast the themes of two stories in a short essay

---

Tip 7

- Make assignments relevant to life to enhance students' motivation and integration of learning.

e.g., Solve this problem: Your parents have told you that you may have new carpeting in your bedroom, but they want you to figure out how much carpeting is needed. Calculate the area of the floor in your bedroom to determine how much new carpeting will be needed.

Tip 8

- Assign different types of homework for variety.

e.g., construct models of three-dimensional geometric shapes

Tip 9

- Individualize homework to accommodate the needs of special populations.

e.g., provide a word bank for an ESOL student's vocabulary worksheet

Tips for Parents

❖ **Create an environment that supports homework.**
- Set a **regular time** for homework (e.g., before dinner).
- Find a **quiet, well lit spot** for completion of homework.
- Provide traditional **supplies** (e.g., pencils/pens/markers, paper, ruler, scissors, glue, etc.) and **technology** (e.g., computer with internet).
- Provide **guidance** by checking to insure your child is completing his/her work and isn't frustrated.
- **Encourage** your child to complete homework and **praise** him/her when the work is completed.

❖ **Work with the teacher to support your child's learning.**
- **Check** your child's homework each day. If there are errors in the homework, have your child fix the error, but don't give him/her the answers.
- Orally **quiz** your child on the content when he/she is studying for a test.
- **Support** your child's completion of a hands-on project by supplying materials and encouragement, but don't do the work for him/her.
- If your child has a homework planner or assignment pad that must be signed by you, **check and sign the planner daily.**
- **Communicate** with your child's teacher about any concerns you have.

Module 8.5
Cooperative Learning

Student Outcomes from Cooperative Learning

Increases Academic Growth
- academic achievement
- long term retention
- higher level thinking skills e.g., critical thinking
- student engagement and reduces "creativity killers"
- comprehension of thought and speech patterns in various disciplines

Courtesy of Fotolia

Enhances Psychological Health
- self-esteem
- self-efficacy
- emotional maturity
- personal identity
- trust in others

Courtesy of Fotolia

Develops Social Skills
- skills in collaborative work
- ability to work effectively with others
- social relations
- liking for others
- respect for those of different racial/cultural backgrounds or disabilities

Courtesy of Fotolia

Improves Discipline
- motivation
- conflict resolution skills
- attitudes toward school and subjects
- drop-out prevention

Enhances Environmental Factors
- interaction among students
- interaction between teachers and students

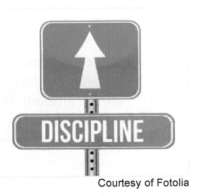

Courtesy of Fotolia

The Components of Cooperative Learning

Introduction

When planning, instructing, and assessing students' learning in cooperative groups, attend to these five components to insure success.

---

1. Positive Interdependence
- ❖ Positive interdependence is when a student learns the required information and completes the assignment but makes sure that everyone else does so as well.
- ❖ Tips for building students' positive interdependence follow.
  - Facilitate group goal setting.
  - Reward and celebrate individual and group successes.
  - Encourage sharing of resources within the groups.
  - Promote group members performing their defined roles.

---

2. Promotive Interaction
- ❖ Promotive interaction means that students interact with one another in ways that build relationships.
- ❖ Tips for fostering students' promotive interaction follow.
  - Provide resources to students.
  - Give specific feedback on students' interactions.
  - Model responsibility and encourage students to act responsibly.
  - Model trustworthiness and encourage trustworthiness in students.

---

3. Accountability and Responsibility
- ❖ When students are accountable to themselves and to their group members for their learning and behavior, they become stronger individuals. This accountability enhances students' sense of responsibility.
- ❖ Tips for developing students' accountability and responsibility follow.
  - Assign groups with a small group size.
  - Test each individual within each group.
  - Randomly examine students orally.
  - Observe the frequency of individuals' participation in groups.
  - Have a student act in the role of "checker" in groups.
  - Use peer tutoring or reciprocal teaching.

4. Social Skills

❖ Social skills are those skills necessary for individuals to get along with others. An example of a social skill for effective participation in cooperative learning is sharing. Another example is giving feedback to a group member in a non-threatening manner.

❖ Tips for encouraging students' social skills follow.

- Build an environment of caring and trust.
- Model effective communication and encourage students to use effective communication too.
- Show acceptance and support toward all students and encourage students to do the same.
- Facilitate constructive conflict resolution within the classroom.

5. Processing

❖ Processing provides the opportunity for a group to reflect on what worked in the group and what didn't in order to enhance the group's effectiveness. Processing is typically done through oral discussion; the group members identify successful processes to continue, areas for improvement, and suggestions for how to improve for the future.

❖ Tips for enhancing students' processing in the classroom follow.

- Provide feedback regarding a group's progress during the early stages of group development.
- Insure that there is time to conduct processing each time the group meets.
- Reward and celebrate each group's successful processes.

Note: The five components of cooperative learning were originally defined by Johnson and Johnson (1994). Please see the *References and Sources* page in this module for further information.

Implementing Cooperative Learning

Introduction

For smooth implementation of cooperative learning, tend to these four tips when planning your lesson.

Tip 1
Choose a cooperative learning method.
- Peer tutoring
- Reciprocal teaching
- Team assisted individualization
- Group investigation
- Student Teams Achievement Divisions (STAD)
- Jigsaw

Tip 2
Determine the number of group members.
- Dyads
- Avoid trios
- Four to six members
- Avoid more than six members
- Multiple layers of groups

Tip 3
Choose a process for selecting group members.
- Self-selection
- Pairing up within categories
- Counting off
- Playing card procedure
- Chalkboard procedure
- Heterogeneous grouping
- Homogeneous grouping

Tip 4
Identify the task.
- Sharing
- Problem solving
- Debating
- Supporting
- Working on a project
- Developing a skill

8.5.3

Tips for Giving Feedback

Introduction

Follow these four tips when giving feedback to your students. The information provided in the tips will help you to facilitate your students' completion of the assigned task while simultaneously enhancing the growth of their academics, psychological health, social skills, and discipline.

Tip 1

Offer feedback using these guidelines.

- Be **patient and gentle**, using an **enthusiastic tone** of voice.
- When giving feedback, **target the behavior, not the person**.
  e.g., "It appears that interrupting is something with which the group is having difficulty."
- Solicit **feedback from the group** members.
  e.g., "What worked for you?" "What helped?" "Where were you heading?" "What are you trying to accomplish?" "What's one way that the group could improve?"

Tip 2

Give specific praise and encouragement.

- Deliver **positive comments first**.
- **Reinforce** what is being done well.
  e.g., "I noticed that you are all following your ground rules." (said with a smile or thumbs up gesture)
- Give **specific praise for the academic tasks** to increase academic performance.
  e.g., "This group completed the assignment with high accuracy. Well done!"
- Use **encouragement** to promote good behavior, social skills, and internal motivation.
  e.g., "It's so nice the way your group stayed on task. You all must feel good about it."

Tip 3

Provide corrective feedback.

- Phrase corrective feedback in a **non-threatening** way.
  e.g., "It would be even more effective if you…."
- Use the feedback to **teach the entire group.**
- Begin corrective feedback with **only one item for improvement the first time.**
- As time passes, you may **increase your corrective feedback as needed.** Starting with only one item allows the group time to identify and correct their own areas for improvement, thus enhancing the group's effectiveness.
  e.g., "You might want to consider reminding each other of the ground rule to make sure that everyone participates, no one dominates."

Tip 4

Intervene only when it is absolutely necessary.

- It's important to **allow students time to work through their own problems.** Therefore, only intervene in the group's work when they are severely stuck.
- **Begin with low level interventions** (see Module 9 for more information) to help the group to remedy their problem. Don't jump in and direct them.
- Try the following process.
  1. Identify the **source of the problem.**
     e.g., Is the problem due to the structure of group membership? Are individuals in the group lacking a social skill?
  2. Identify the **intervention.**
     e.g., Can the membership be reconstructed? Can strong members in the group be asked to coach those having problems?

Courtesy of Fotolia

8.5.4

Tips for Assisting Cooperative Learning Groups

Introduction

Try these three tips for assisting cooperative learning groups to function more successfully.

Tip 1
Get students to agree from the very beginning. Examples follow.
- What are the group's **ground rules** or norms for behavior?
  e.g., class rules
- How will the group **make decisions**?
  e.g., consensus, voting with everyone agreeing to support the final vote
- What is everyone's **role**?
  e.g., recorder, materials manager, etc.
- What will be the group's **outcomes**?
  e.g., pass a vocabulary quiz, finish a science project
- What is the **agenda** for each group meeting?
  e.g., set goals to achieve outcomes

Courtesy of Fotolio

Tip 2
Model, teach, and use effective communication skills.
- **Model** effective communication skills (see Module 9).
- Provide students **instruction and practice** so that they develop effective communication skills.
- Provide **feedback** on students' use of their effective communication skills.

Tip 3
Reinforce decisions, duties, and deadlines.

- **Continuously check for agreements on decisions.**
  A student can be assigned the role of "Checker" to insure that the group continuous checks their decisions.
  e.g., "Can we all agree on this?" or "We all agree with _____, right?"

- **Identify each person's duties.**
  Identifying duties means that each individual has a role in the group with assigned duties that help the group to achieve its outcomes. Periodically review each person's role and job.

- **Immediately establish deadlines for completion of work and stick to those deadlines.**
  Be sure to build in a little extra time just in case there is an unforeseen problem. Revisit the timeline regularly so that everyone knows when their respective tasks/jobs are due.

Activity 15: Solving Problems with Cooperative Learning

Directions:

Review the information in this module; then, using the information, generate **two to three solutions** for each problem posed. Remember that one of the purposes of cooperative learning is to develop students' cooperative skills, so some of your solutions should reflect your efforts to facilitate those skills. **Record** your solutions to each problem here. Be sure to **submit** the final product to your instructor on the due date.

Problem # 1
Two students in the same group keep gossiping and hardly do any work.

Problem # 2
The groups aren't getting cleaned up on time.

Problem # 3
One dyad in the class isn't working out. One member is doing all the work.

Problem # 4
The expert groups are not functioning as well as they could. It appears that the strongest students academically are doing most of the work.

Problem # 5
One group is not consistently taking time to do group processing.

Problem #6

One project group is heading in the wrong direction; they are not addressing the assignment that was given.

Problem #7

Two students from the same group come to you at different times complaining about each other.

Problem #8

Not all the group members are learning the assigned material.

Problem #9

A new student arrives after the home groups have been working together for three weeks.

Problem #10

One of the groups for the group investigation of vertebrates has all low achieving students in it. The group can't seem to get organized and is having difficulty reading the necessary material.

Module 8.6
Problem-based Instruction

Implementing Problem-based Instruction

Introduction

Problem-based Instruction helps students to explore **real-life problems or questions** that require them to learn knowledge in **multiple subjects** simultaneously. The model emphasizes **inductive reasoning** that you, as the teacher, facilitate by scaffolding students' learning. Like cooperative learning, problem-based instruction requires that **students are actively involved** in the learning process. Students may work individually or in small groups on a problem or question that sparks their interest. They answer the problem or question by completing a project or analyzing a case and generate a product to demonstrate learning.

Projects are composed of a series of tasks that result in an answer to the problem or question posed and result in a product.

For **example**, a science fair project investigates a problem or answers a question using the scientific method (e.g., What are the effects of oil spills on the ocean?). The problem or question requires the student to explore and use knowledge from multiple subjects, such as mathematics, marine biology, environmental science, etc. The student follows the steps in the scientific method in order to draw a conclusion that proposes a solution to the problem or answers the question. The student presents the completed project to demonstrate learning.

Courtesy of Fotolia

Courtesy of Fotolio

Cases may be vignettes, scenarios, simulations, or even legal briefs that present a problem or question.

For **example**, students may be required to read a case that describes an ethical dilemma. The dilemma may require them to explore and use knowledge in philosophy, psychology, law, etc. The students then analyze the case following a series of steps (see Module 8.6.2) and share the action plan that they develop in order to resolve the ethical dilemma.

Tips for Success with Problem-based Instruction

Tip 1

Select a high-interest topic.

- Consider using something that is currently an **issue in the news** (e.g., environmental clean-up of an oil spill, a case that will be heard by the Supreme Court, etc.).
- **Ask the students** what interests them, either from your pre-selected topics or ask them to generate their own topics.
- Ensure that the topic is part of the **state standards** for the grade level.

Tip 2

Scaffold the learning.

- Identify the **subject areas** from which students will draw knowledge to solve the problem or answer the question.
- Give students a **step-by-step process** for completing the project or solving the case.
- Provide students with a **timeline** for completion, including due dates for each step of the process they will use to complete the project or case.
- Communicate your expectations for learning by providing a **grading rubric** for the completed product.
- Consider using **group processing** for groups of students who work together on the project or case to enhance group effectiveness.
- **Supervise** students and provide **feedback** during each stage of the learning process.

Tip 3

Assess the learning.

- Schedule time for students to **present** their products.
- Use the **grading rubric** to assess if students have met your expectations for learning.
- Provide **feedback on the product and process**—specific praise, encouragement, and constructive criticism.

Process for Solving a Case

Introduction

Have your students follow these seven steps to effectively solve a case.

Step 1
Become familiar with the case.
- The students thoroughly **read the case and related material**. Related material may include assigned readings from a variety of subject areas that have pertinent information for solving the case.

Courtesy of Fotolia

Step 2
Identify potential problems.
- The students **brainstorm** what they think the problems are in the case study.
- **Brainstorming** means generating as many ideas as possible—in this case ideas about what the potential problems are in the case. Also, ideas must be generated without negative comments or criticism. However, students may add to someone else's idea.
- Next, the students **clarify** the list of problems. When clarifying, students **pose questions** about any brainstormed problems they don't understand. The purpose of clarifying is to make sure that everyone clearly comprehends the items in the list. Simply **rewording** items in the list is sometimes all it takes to clarify a brainstormed problem.

Step 3
Identify common themes.
- The students review the list of brainstormed sources of the problem and identify **common themes or categories of ideas**.
- Next, the students **label** the categories. Depending on the case presented and the list brainstormed, there may be anywhere from two to ten different categories.

Step 4

Create problem statements and select a problem to solve.

- The students create a problem statement for each theme or category of problems by **synthesizing** the items in that theme or category. The problem statement should begin with the phrase: **"The problem is how to. . ."**

- Then, the students **select** a problem to solve. Students vote on which problem they would like to solve, and the problem with the most votes is selected. In the case of a tie, the students revote to break the tie.

Courtesy of Fotolia

Step 5

Brainstorm solutions.

- The students **brainstorm** solutions for the selected problem.

- Next, the students **clarify** the list of solutions.

Step 6

Condense, evaluate, and select the solutions.

- The students condense or **reduce** the list of solutions. For example, some solutions may be combined into one solution by adding the word "and." Also, the solutions may be condensed into common themes or categories.

- Next, the students **review** and **evaluate** the solutions **based on specific criteria**. Consider using the following questions/criteria to facilitate your students' evaluation of their solutions.

  Question 1: What are the **implications** of the solution?
    - ✓ legal
    - ✓ ethical
    - ✓ moral
    - ✓ social
    - ✓ political
    - ✓ economic

  Question 2: Based on the implications, is the solution **feasible**?

- The students then **select** their top solution by voting.

Step 7

Develop an action plan.

- The students may develop an action plan to carry out the solution to the problem. An **action plan** identifies each step that must be taken in order to implement the solution to solve the identified problem.

Note. You may want your students to select the top two or three solutions and develop action plans for them. In this way, students learn about contingency planning—having a back-up in case the first solution doesn't work.

Courtesy of Fotolia

Activity 16: Solving Problems with Problem-based Instruction

Directions:

Review the information in this module; then, using the information, generate **two to three solutions** for each problem posed. You will find that some of the issues that arise in problem-based instruction are similar to those of cooperative learning. Also, remember that one of the purposes of problem-based instruction is to develop students' inductive reasoning skills, so some of your solutions should reflect your efforts to scaffold students' learning. **Record** your solutions to each problem here. Remember to **submit** the final product to your instructor on the due date.

Problem # 1
The students have difficulty evaluating their solutions so that they can select one.

Problem # 2
One of your student groups is having difficulty with timely completion of the step-by-step process for their project. They are not meeting the timeline that you set.

Problem # 3
When students begin brainstorming potential problems in the case you have assigned, one student keeps criticizing other students' ideas.

Problem # 4
Several students haven't done the required reading for the discussion of the case.

Problem # 5
Your students are working on their science fair projects, and you notice that several of them aren't using the grading rubric as a guide for their work.

Problem #6
You have split your students into small groups and assigned them cases to solve. One of the groups isn't following the process for solving a case, and is bogged down in arguing about the potential problems.

Problem #7
Your students are trying to categorize their brainstormed items but don't seem to understand how to do so.

Problem #8
One student complains that he isn't interested in the topic that the class has selected for their project.

Module 8.7
Discussion and Recitation

Guidelines for Recitation

Introduction

The information in these pages defines recitation, shares the outcomes of its proper use, explains questions by type and complexity, explains how to pose questions and handle student responses successfully, and provides tips for how to motivate students with questions.

I. What is recitation?

Recitation is a teaching method that is used both to **instruct students and monitor their learning**. You, as the teacher, pose a question; then, you call on a student to answer the question. The process is repeated until you have posed enough questions to stimulate and/or monitor students' learning.

II. What are the outcomes of recitation?

The **outcomes** for students when you ask well-constructed questions during recitation are
- increased involvement,
- enhanced thinking,
- development of a questioning attitude, and
- heightened motivation for further learning.

Courtesy of Fotolia

III. What are the types of questions for recitation?

Type 1: Questions that Seek Information
  1. **Definitions**
     e.g., What is the definition of a mammal?
  2. **Facts**
     e.g., Who delivered the *Gettysburg Address*?
  3. **Judgments**
     e.g., Based on what you learned about the five food groups, what constitutes a healthy diet?
  4. **Preferences**
     e.g., What did the Pilgrims value above all else?
  5. **Processes**
     e.g., How do you check the answer to an addition problem?

Type 2: Questions that Call for Analysis
  1. **Assumptions**
     e.g., What contextual factors did you use when solving the problem?
  2. **Conclusions**
     e.g., How are the two main characters in the story alike?
  3. **Connections**
     e.g., Given our study of eating for healthy living, what connections can you make between diet and obesity?
  4. **Consequences**
     e.g., What are the potential effects of industries dumping waste chemicals into waterways?
  5. **Ideas**
     e.g., What would happen if the main character made a different decision during the climax of the story?
  6. **Inferences**
     e.g., Based on the material we read, what can you infer was the cause of the Black Plague?
  7. **Perspectives**
     e.g., What viewpoint did you use when you answered the question about what makes a good sneaker?
  8. **Predictions**
     e.g., What would happen if you decreased the amount of light that the plant was exposed to each day?
  9. **Verifications**
     e.g., What evidence supports the conclusion that you drew from your experiment?

IV. When are closed and open-ended questions used?

- Use **closed questions** for **recall** of content that has a **specific correct answer**. These questions typically seek information, as those described previously.
- Follow these **tips** to use closed questions successfully.
  - ✓ Require students to recall prior knowledge.
  - ✓ Ask about concrete, specific, and familiar facts and/or concepts.
  - ✓ Paraphrase an answer to a previously asked question as a follow-up question.
  - ✓ Include probes and hints for the students as needed.
  - ✓ Consider asking these questions within a game context to motivate students.

- Use **open-ended questions** to require **critical and creative thinking** and accept **multiple answers**. These questions typically require analysis, as those described previously.
- Follow these **tips** to use open-ended questions successfully.
  - ✓ Ask your students to generalize information and use it in a new context to answer the question.
  - ✓ Look for multiple answers.
  - ✓ Require your students to clarify and justify the reasons for their answers.
  - ✓ Ask questions about complex concepts and generalizations.

Courtesy of Fotolia

V. How are questions asked and students' responses handled?

Tip 1

Pose the question.
- ✓ Alert students that you are asking a question by using marker expressions (e.g., "Get ready!" or "This is an important question!")
- ✓ Ask only one question at a time. Doing so avoids confusion.
- ✓ Vary the questions by type in order to promote thinking and learning.
- ✓ To insure that students hear the question, you may repeat the question as needed, but alert that students that you are doing so.
- ✓ If students don't seem to understand the question, consider rephrasing it, but alert students that you are doing so.

Tip 2

Use wait-time.
- ✓ Pose a question and then **wait 3-5 seconds** before calling on a student to respond. Using wait-time allows students a chance to reflect on the question and think about a response.

Tip 3

Acknowledge correct responses.
- ✓ Employ **specific praise** to recognize a student's correct response.
- ✓ Use **body language** to acknowledge correct responses. e.g., smiles, thumbs up

Courtesy of Fotolia

Tip 4

Employ follow-up questions.
- ✓ After a student's response, pose a **probing question** that asks the student to clarify and/or elaborate on the response. Posing a follow-up question allows for additional processing of the content.

Tip 5

Handle incorrect or partially correct responses.

Students may give a response that: is incorrect; may be partially correct; or follows the correct line of thought, but does not give the correct answer. When these situations occur, try some of the following tips to promote learning.

- ✓ Provide a hint or prompt.
- ✓ Ask if the student would like someone else to assist him/her.
- ✓ Recognize the portion of the answer or thought that is correct.
- ✓ Supply the question for which an incorrect answer would be correct.
- ✓ Hold the student accountable by saying that you know he/she will answer the question correctly next time.

Tip 6

Be aware of your students' cultural and language differences and accommodate differences.

Different cultures use

- different lengths of wait time,
- varying paces of conversation, and
- various levels of formality and participation between a teacher and students.

Tip 7

Support student motivation.

- ✓ Provide silent think time.
- ✓ Have students share their answers with a partner before answering.
- ✓ Ask students to record their responses in their notebooks or journals.
- ✓ Request that students raise their hands when they have a related answer.
- ✓ Use questions to refocus ideas.
- ✓ Clarify misunderstandings.
- ✓ Avoid saying "No." to a student's response that is incorrect; may be partially correct; or follows the correct line of thought, but does not give the correct answer. Use the tips described previously to help the student avoid embarrassment.

Generating a Guiding Question

I. What is a guiding question?

A **guiding question** is a query that is designed for the purpose of promoting the study of a topic. It is an **open-ended** question that requires **analysis**. Answering the question requires student to examine and synthesize content on the topic in order to answer the question.

II. What are the characteristics of a guiding question?

Guiding questions must adhere to the following characteristics in order to be effective for a discussion lesson.

- **Clearly word** the question. Use language that your students will understand.
- Make the question **concise and brief**. It should be short and sweet!
- Confirm that the question is **non-judgmental**. It doesn't lead the students in one direction or another.
- Ensure that the question **brings focus** to the topic. It needs to invite discussion by concentrating on one concern, issue, or problem.
- Pose a question that is **intellectually challenging** and **promotes higher level thinking**. The question should require students to analyze, evaluate, and create.
- Make certain that the question **sparks passion**. When the question has emotive force, it also arouses motivation!

Courtesy of Fotolia

Module 8 References and Sources

Arends, R. I. (2012). *Learning to teach* (9th ed.). New York: McGraw-Hill.

Bertucci, A., Meloni, C., Conti, S., & Carellini, L. (2005). The role of personality, gender and interaction in a cooperative and in a computer supported collaborative learning task. *Journal of Science Education, 6*, 32-36.

Borich, G. D., (2014). *Effective teaching methods* (8th ed.). Upper Saddle River, NJ: Pearson.

Baker, M. (2010-2013). *Useful charts publishing: Classification of animals and living things.* Retrieved from http://www.usefulcharts.com/science/classification-of-animals-chart.html

Burden, P. R., & Byrd, D. M. (2013). *Methods for effective teaching: Meeting the needs of all students* (6th ed.). Boston: Allyn & Bacon.

Campbell, L., Campbell, B., & Dickenson, D. (2004). *Teaching and learning through multiple intelligences* (3rd ed.). Upper Saddle River, NJ: Pearson.

Carson, L., & Hoyle, S. (1990). Teaching social skills: A view from the classroom. *Educational Leadership, 47*(4), 31.

Child Development Project. (1988). Portrait of the child development project. *Working Together, 17*, 1-10.

Collins, D. W., Purdom, D. M., & Fardig, G. E. (1985). *Teaching concepts. Activities 3 and 5.* Tallahassee, FL: Florida State Department of Education.

Cornelius-White, J. (2007). Learner-centered teacher-student relationships are effective: A meta-analysis. *Review of Educational Research, 77*(1), 113-143.

Courtney, D. P., Courtney, M., & Nicholson, C. (1992). *The effect of cooperative learning as an instructional practice at the college level.* (ERIC Document Reproduction Service No. ED 354 808.)

DLTK. (1998-2013). *Kidzone science: Animal classes.* Retrieved from http://www.kidzone.ws/animals/animal_classes.htm

Dockterman, D. A. (1998). *Cooperative learning and technology.* Watertown, MA: Tom Snyder Productions.

Dunlap, L. L. (1997). *An introduction to early childhood special education.* Boston: Allyn & Bacon.

Elder, L., & Paul, R. (2002). *The miniature guide to the art of asking essential questions.* Dillon Beach, CA: Foundation for Critical Thinking.

Estes, T. H., Mintz, S. L., & Gunter, M. A., (2011). *Instruction: A models approach* (6th ed.) Upper Saddle River, NJ: Pearson.

Flannery, J. L. (1994). Teacher as co-conspirator: Knowledge and authority in collaborative learning. *New Directions for Teaching and Learning, 59*, 15-23.

Forest, L. (2001). *Crafting creative community: combining cooperative learning, multiple intelligences, and nature's wisdom.* San Clemente, CA: Kagan.

Fosnot, C. T. (1989). *Enquiring teachers, enquiring learners: A constructivist approach for teaching.* New York: Teaches College Press.

Freiberg, J. H. (1996). From tourists to citizens in the classroom. *Educational Leadership, 54*(1), 32-36.

Gartner, A. J., & Riessman, F. (1994). Tutoring helps to those who give, those who receive. *Educational Leadership, 52*(3), 58-60.

Gill, P. B., & Essien-Barrett, B. (2000, February). *Can we model what we teach? A cooperative approach to constructivist pedagogy.* Paper presented at the Annual Conference of Association of Teacher Educators, Orlando, Florida.

Grenier, M., Dyson, B., & Yeaton, P. (2005). Cooperative learning that includes students with disabilities. *Journal of Physical Education, Recreation and Dance, 76*(6) 29-35.

Guyton, E. (1991). Cooperative learning and elementary social studies. *Social Education, 55*(5), 313-315.

Hersey, P., Blanchard, K. H., & Johnson, D. E. (2013). *Management of organizational behavior* (10th ed.). Upper Saddle River, NJ: Pearson.

Holloway, J. H. (2003/2004). Student teamwork. *Educational Leadership, 61*(4), 91-92.

Interaction Associates. (1988). *Facilitative leadership trainer's guide.* San Francisco, CA: Author.

Jacobs, G. M., Power, M. A., & Loh, W. I. (2002). *The teacher's sourcebook for cooperative learning: Practical techniques, basic principles, and frequently asked questions.* Thousand Oaks, CA: Corwin Press.

Jenkins, J. R., Antil, L. R., Wayne, S. K., & Vadasy, P. F. (2003). How cooperative learning works for special education and remedial students. *Exceptional Children, 69*(3), 279-292.

Johnson, D. W., & Johnson, R. T. (1990). Social skills for successful group work. *Educational Leadership, 47*(4), 29-33.

Johnson, D. W., & Johnson, R. T. (1994). An overview of cooperative learning. In J. S. Thousand, R. A. Villa, & A. I. Nevin (Eds.). *Creativity and collaborative learning: A practical guide to empowering students and teachers* (pp. 31-44). Baltimore, MD: Paul H. Brookes.

Johnson, S. W., & Johnson, R. T. (2009). The importance of social and emotional learning In P. R. LeBlanc & N. P. Gallavan (Eds.), *Affective teacher education: Exploring connections among knowledge, skills, and dispositions* (pp. 1-26). NY: Rowman & Littlefield.

Johnson, D. W., & Johnson, R. T. (2013). *Joining together: Group theory and group skills* (11th ed.). Boston: Allyn & Bacon.

Johnson, D. W, Johnson, R. T., & Holubec, E. J. (2002). *Circles of learning: Cooperation in the classroom* (5th ed.). Edina, MN: Interaction Book Company.

Johnson, D. W, Johnson, R. T., & Smith, K. (1991). *Cooperative learning: Increasing college faculty instructional productivity.* ASHE-ERIC Reports on Higher Education. Washington, DC. (ERIC Document Reproduction Service No. ED343465)

Johnson, D. W, Johnson, R. T., & Smith, K. (1998). *Active learning: Cooperation in the college classroom.* Edine, MN: Interaction Book Company.

Johnson, D. W., Johnson, R. T., & Stanne, M. B. (2000). *Cooperative learning methods: A meta-analysis.* Retrieved from http://www.clcrc.com/pages/cl-methods.html

Jutras, P. F. (1994). *Developing students' capacity for learning and thinking through integrated curriculum and team learning experiences.* (ERIC Document Reproduction Service No. ED376788)

LeBlanc, P. R., & Skaruppa, C. (1997). Support for democratic schooling: Classroom level change via cooperative learning. *Action in Teacher Education, 19*(1), 28-38.

Lemming, J. S. (1992). The influence of contemporary issues curricula on school-aged youth. In C. Grant (Ed.). *Review of research in education* (pp. 111-116). Washington, DC: American Educational Research Association.

Mandel, S. M. (2003). *Cooperative work groups: Preparing students for the real world.* Thousand Oaks, CA: Corwin Press.

Manning, M. L., & Lucking, R. (1991). The what, why, and how of cooperative learning. *The Social Studies, 82*(3), 120-124.

McCracken, P. (2005). Cooperative learning as a classroom management strategy. *Momentum, 36*(4), 10-12.

Morrison, G. R., Ross, S. M., & Kemp, J. E. (2004). *Designing effective instruction* (4th ed.). Indianapolis, IN: John Wiley & Sons.

Murray, F. B. (1994). Why understanding the theoretical basis of cooperative learning enhances teaching success. In J. S. Thousand, R. A. Villa, & A. I. Nevin (Eds.). *Creativity and collaborative learning: A practical guide to empowering students and teachers* (pp. 3-11). Baltimore, MD: Paul H. Brookes.

National Education Association (n.d.). *Research spotlight on homework.* Retrieved from http://www.nea.org/tools/16938.htm

Nevin, A. I., Smith, K. A., & Udvari-Solner, A. (1994). Cooperative group learning and higher education. In J. S. Thousand, R. A. Villa, & A. I. Nevin (Eds.). *Creativity and collaborative learning: A practical guide to empowering students and teachers* (pp. 115-127). Baltimore, MD: Paul H. Brookes.

Paulu, N. (1998). *Helping your students with homework: A guide for teachers.* Washington, D.C.: U.S. Department of Education. Retrieved from http://www.ed.gov/pubs/HelpingStudents/index.html

Pearson, Inc. (200-2013). *Fact monster: Scientific classification.* Retrieved from http://www.factmonster.com/ipka/A0193009.html

Dabbagh, N. (2002-2006). *The instructional design knowledge base: Perform a task analysis.* Retrieved from http://classweb.gmu.edu/ndabbagh/Resources/IDKB/index.htm

Dabbagh, N. (2002-2006). *The instructional design knowledge base: Procedural task analysis.* Retrieved from http://classweb.gmu.edu/ndabbagh/Resources/IDKB/index.htm

Rothstein-Fisch, C., Trumbull, E., Isaac, A., Daley, C., & Perez, A. I. (2003). When "helping someone else" is the right answer: Bridging cultures in assessment. *Journal of Latinos and Education, 2*(3), 123-140.

Schneider, E. (1996). Giving students a voice in the classroom. *Educational Leadership, 54*(1), 22-26.

Schwartz, N., Gonzalez-Smith, V., Downie, D. E., Cannon, E., Cota, J., Garrison Jordan C., Henderson, M. G., Kennedy, J., Pellicano, J., Carlson, D. L., & Bullion, P. (1995). A team approach to cooperative learning. *Teaching and Change, 2*(2), 118-140.

Slavin, R. E. (1990). Research on cooperative learning: Consensus and controversy. *Educational Leadership, 47*(4), 52-55.

Slavin, R. E. (1991). Synthesis of research on cooperative learning. *Phi Delta Kappan, 48*(5), 71-82.

Study Guides and Strategies. (n.d.). *Problem-based instruction.* Retrieved from http://www.studygs.net/pbl.htm

Tate, M. L. (2003). *Worksheets don't grow dendrites: 20 instructional strategies that engage the brain.* Thousand Oaks, CA: Corwin Press.

Thousand, J. S., Villa, R. A., & Nevin, A. (2002). *Creativity and collaborative learning: the practical guide to empowering students, teachers, and families* (2nd ed.). Baltimore, MD: Paul H. Brookes Publishers.

U.S. Department of Education (n.d.). *A teacher's guide to homework tips for parents.* Retrieved from http://www.ed.gov/teachers/how/parents/homework-tips/edlite-index.html

U.S. Department of Education (2005). *Helping your child with homework* (rev. ed.). Washington, D.C.: Author. Retrieved from http://www2.ed.gov/parents/academic/help/homework/

Wiley & Sons. (2013). *For dummies. Categorizing mother nature: The Linnaean Taxonomic System.* Retrieved from http://www.dummies.com/how-to/content/categorizing-mother-nature-the-linnaean-taxonomic-.html

Module 9
Classroom Management

Purpose of Classroom Management

Courtesy of Fotolia

Classroom management refers to the actions that teachers take in order to insure that students learn in a **safe instructional environment**. These actions are described in detail in the classroom management course for your major. However, classroom management is included here so that you will have a grasp of some of the basics needed for you to successfully instruct students.

Some of the classroom management concerns to which you must pay attention when planning for instruction include the following areas.

- Arranging seating
- Managing materials
- Effective communication
- Preventions
- Classroom rules
- Praise and encouragement
- Potential rewards
- Discipline hierarchy
- Interventions
- Desisting inappropriate behavior

Tips for Effective Communication

Introduction

Effective communication involves speaking, listening, responding, and non-verbal messages. Follow the tips for each of these areas to ensure that you are communicating effectively. Modeling these behaviors will help teach your students effective communication.

I. Speaking

Tip 1
Know when to speak.

- Respond when appropriate. Respond to the idea and not the person.
e.g., Try: "I'm not sure that your idea works in this situation. Could you tell me more about it?"

Tip 2
Be non-evaluative or use neutral framing.

- Say what you perceive the person's actions to be rather than making a negative statement.
e.g., Use: "You're interrupting me."
Avoid: "You're rude."

Tip 3
Use clarity.

- If the receiver is a child, explain the information in a way that a child will understand.
  - e.g., Try: "I am so happy that you have earned a grade of A on your final Science test!"
- Don't use educational jargon with parents.
Avoid: "You met the benchmark for Science this academic year."
e.g., Use: "Your child has achieved the goal in Science for his grade level."
Avoid: "Your child has met the benchmark for Science this academic year."

Courtesy of Fotolia

Tip 4

Ask questions and seek feedback.

- Ask the person receiving your message for input on what his/her interpretations of your communication are.

e.g., Try: "Would you please share your understanding of what I just said?"

Tip 5

Demonstrate personal ownership.

- Use "I" and "my" statements.

e.g., State: "I don't appreciate that you are shouting at me, and I want you to stop shouting now."

Tip 6

Describe your feelings.

- Using "I" language, say how you feel. Use descriptive, feeling words.

e.g., Try: "It makes me very sad when you do not do your homework. I want you to do your best."

Tip 7

Repeat if needed.

- Say the message more than once. Rephrase it. Use more than one form of communication.

e.g., Pose the query: "What were the effects of European colonization on the Native American tribes in Florida?"

Rephrase the query: "What happened to the Native American tribes in Florida because of European colonization?"

II. Listening and Responding

Tip 1

Show your comprehension.

- Demonstrate your comprehension by paraphrasing what has been said.

e.g., Student says: "I want to practice my math facts at home when I have more time."

Restate: "I hear you saying that you would have more time to study if you rehearse your math facts at home."

Tip 2
Tell the speaker what you perceive are his/her feelings.
- Paraphrase your perceptions of the speaker's feelings. Try stating your perceptions as question to seek clarification.
e.g., Try: "Are you feeling…?"

Tip 3
Tell what you think the speaker is saying.
- Share what you think by paraphrasing.
e.g., Use: "What I think you mean is…"

Tip 4
Negotiate.
- Give and take in communication resolves conflicts so that each person "wins" and the relationship is maintained.
e.g., Try: "How about if I use the blue marker now, and you use the red marker first?"

Tip 5
Know when to refuse.
- Say "no" gracefully.
e.g., Use: "As much as I would love to join the committee, I wouldn't be able to do a good job because I am already on another committee. Thank you for asking me though!"

Courtesy of Fotolia

9.2

III. Non-verbal Messages

Tip 1
Use appropriate eye contact, facial expressions, body posture, and gestures.
- Know what is appropriate. Respect traditions and understand cultural differences.

e.g., Make eye contact with your students while you are teaching. Scan the room to do so. Stand tall and use body language to convey enthusiasm for the lesson.

e.g., Touch students only on the upper arm. Hugs can be misconstrued. Touching the top of a student's head may violate a religious belief.

Tip 2
Use appropriate voice tone and levels.
- Modulate the tone and volume of your voice as appropriate to the setting. Avoid angry, loud outbursts.

e.g., As you approach a misbehaving student, say in a soft tone with a low volume: "I want you to stop fidgeting in your seat. Your behavior is distracting others."

Tip 3
Be congruent.
- Match your non-verbal and verbal communication.

e.g., Greet a parent at your classroom door with a smile, open body posture, and a hand shake saying, "Welcome to the classroom. I am happy to see you."

Courtesy of Fotolia

Preventions

Preventions are the strategies that you use, as a teacher, to stop misbehavior before it starts. Listed below are the areas to which you must attend to successfully prevent most misbehavior. In this way, you and the students will be able to focus on instruction in a safe environment.

❖ Use effective communication skills.
❖ Arrange students' seating as appropriate for the instructional model you use (see module 8.1).
❖ Manage your materials effectively (see Module 3).
❖ Develop clear and easy to follow classroom rules.
❖ Continuously monitor students' behavior and learning.
❖ Employ specific praise and encouragement.
❖ Provide rewards and guidelines for attaining them.
❖ Consistently enforce the classroom rules.
❖ Intervene to correct misbehavior behavior.
❖ Desist inappropriate behavior.
❖ Provide consequences for rule infractions with a discipline hierarchy.
❖ Consistently deliver consequences for rule infractions.

Courtesy of Fotolia

Tips for Creating Classroom Rules

Introduction

Follow these tips to ensure that you have classroom rules that are clear and students will follow.

Courtesy of Fotolia

Tip 1

Make your rules practical.

❖ Be sure that the rule is something that is appropriate for the age and grade level of your students.

Ask These Questions:
- Is this rule something that students will be able to follow?
- Is the rule developmentally appropriate?

Example Rule: Remain seated during instruction.

Answers to Questions:
- Students in the early elementary grades may have difficulty with this rule if there are no breaks for movement between instructional activities. Most upper elementary age students, middle school, and high school students will be able to follow this rule.
- Please keep in mind that the average adult can attend for only 20 minutes, so be sure to structure your instructional activities accordingly.

Tip 2

Have rationales for your rules.

❖ Explain the reason why each rule is important. Make sure that the students understand both the rules and rationales for them so that they will be motivated to follow the rules.

Courtesy of Fotolia

Ask These Questions:

- Is this rule vitally important?
- How will it enhance the learning of students?

Example Rule: Only one person speaks at a time.
Rationale: This rule is important so that everyone can hear and understand who is speaking and shows respect for the speaker.

Answers to Questions:

- This rule prevents multiple people from talking at the same time; thus, it avoids chaos, too much noise, and disrespect for others.
- Students will be better able to concentrate and learn if only one person speaks at a time.

Tip 3

Make your rules well-constructed; they should be

(a) brief,

(b) few in number, and

(c) clearly and positively worded.

❖ If the rules are brief and few in number, students will be better able to remember them. Using clear, grade level appropriate language makes the rules understandable. Also, rules need to be worded positively so that students know the behavior that they must perform. For example, say: "Walk." rather than "Don't run." Children tend not to hear the "don't" or "not."

Courtesy of Fotolia

Ask These Questions:

- Is this rule vitally important?
- How will it enhance the learning of students?
- Are there only about five rules?
- Are my rules written in short sentences?
- Are the rules written in language that the students can understand?
- Did I avoid the use of "no" and "not"?

Example Rule: Be respectful to everyone and everything.

Answers to Questions:

- The rule is essential.
- It promotes learning by maintaining a caring instructional environment where students feel it is safe to make mistakes.
- This rule is one of only five rules.
- The rule is a short sentence.
- The rule is written in vocabulary that the students will understand.
- The rule uses positive terms.

Tip 4

Be sure that your rules align with the school's rules.

❖ Students need to understand that the rules of the school and classroom are important and that following them keeps all students learning in a safe environment.

Courtesy of Fotolia

Ask These Questions:

- What are the school rules?
- Do my classroom rules fit well with the school's rules?

Example Rule: Keep hands, feet, and objects to yourself.

Answers to Questions:

- School rules prohibit pushing, kicking, fighting, stealing, etc.
- This classroom rule positively states the behavior necessary in both the classroom and school in order to have a safe environment.

Praise and Encouragement

Introduction

The following chart identifies terms, definitions, and examples of applications in the classroom for how to deliver praise and encouragement. Remember that praise and encouragement must be appropriate for the grade level of the students in order for it to be effective.

Terms	Definitions	Examples
▪ Specific praise	▪ Specific praise promotes responsibility when it is personal, genuine, descriptive, specific, and age appropriate.	▪ "Good, Juan. You went right to work on your essay."
▪ Appreciative	▪ Appreciative praise describes the students' academic achievement.	▪ "I found the descriptive words that you used in your essay particularly effective."
▪ Evaluative, global or general praise INEFFECTIVE	▪ Evaluative praise is vague and considered INEFFECTIVE.	▪ "Great job!" INEFFECTIVE
▪ Encouragement	▪ Encouragement is words and actions that convey the teacher's respect and belief in the student's abilities. It recognizes effort or behavior, not achievement. ▪ Encouragement promotes students' development of responsible behavior. ▪ Encouragement urges students to do the best they can.	▪ "Tamika, when you help distribute supplies so quickly and quietly, I'm very pleased because we can get all our work done on time." ▪ "The bell will ring soon. I appreciate your help with straightening up the room for the next class." ▪ "I can tell that you have been working really hard on your essay."
▪ Affirmation	▪ Affirmations are positive statements to students that recognize positive traits.	▪ "I have noticed your thoughtfulness."
▪ Appreciation	▪ Appreciation shows the teacher's pride in the students' accomplishments or behavior.	▪ "I'm proud of you for earning a grade of A on your essay."

Potential Rewards

Introduction

Positive behavior, either academic or social-emotional, can be reinforced using rewards if the item appeals to the student. Remember that the rewards must be appropriate for the grade level of the students. The lists provided here contain sample items that potentially can be used with students. To add to the lists, try the following tips.

- Have the students complete an interest inventory with likes/dislikes identified.
- Have the students brainstorm to generate rewards that interest them.

Courtesy of Fotolia

Intangible Rewards

Courtesy of Fotolia

Privileges and Activities

Class messenger	Line caboose	Read a comic book
Distribute paper	Line leader	Serve as secretary for class meetings
Decorate the bulletin board	Line up first	Sit with a friend
Do puzzles	Make up a funny song	Take attendance
Draw a picture	Message a friend	Talk quietly with a friend
Erase the whiteboard	Nerf or beach ball throw	Teacher pantomimes
Extra computer time	No homework pass	Tell a joke
Feed the class pet	Paint a picture	Visit the media center/library
Free time	Paper passer	Water the plants
Hold the classroom door	Play a game	Work with clay

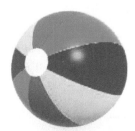

Courtesy of Fotolia

Courtesy of Fotolia

Courtesy of Fotolia

Tangible Rewards

Courtesy of Fotolia

Food
- Be sure to use small amounts and avoid sugary items as much as possible to promote students' eating for healthy living.
- Also, be aware of students' food allergies.
- Avoid all nuts, as it is one of the most frequent and severe food allergies in children.

Beverages: juice pouches/boxes, diet soft drinks	Crackers: animal, graham, cheese, oyster, etc.	Minis: cupcakes, marshmallows
Candy: kisses, M&M's, small sized bars, small lollypops	Dried fruits: raisins, cranberries, blueberries, apricots, etc.	Popcorn
Cereal	Fruit: sliced apples, bananas, oranges, etc.	Popsicles (sugar free)
Chips (small bags)	Ice cream bars	Pretzels
Cookies (small sizes)	Jello or pudding cups (sugar free)	Yogurt pops

Courtesy of Fotolia

Courtesy of Fotolia

- Consider saving toys given free with children's meals at restaurants.
- When purchasing items, shop at dollar stores, party stores, and discount houses to save money.
- Some companies sell goods in large quantities at a discount. Try searching online.

Balls	Drawing Paper	Pencil holders
Book covers	Flash cards	Pencil sharpeners
Bookmarkers	Flashlights	Pictures/posters
Books	Hair clips/bands	Pins
Buttons	Jacks	Plastic toys
Calendars	Jump ropes	Puzzles
Clay/play dough	Marbles	Stickers
Coloring books	Miniature cars/trucks	Storybooks
Combs/brushes	Paintbrushes	Stuffed animals
Commercial games	Paints	Surprise packages
Crayons	Pens	Toy jewelry
Dolls	Pencils	Yo-yos

Courtesy of Fotolia

Courtesy of Fotolia

Courtesy of Fotolia

Discipline Hierarchy

Introduction

A viable classroom management plan must include a discipline hierarchy. These pages define a discipline hierarchy, give a sample discipline hierarchy, and present information about your behavior and that of your students related to the hierarchy.

> ## Discipline Hierarchy Defined
> ✓ A hierarchy lists the consequences for misbehavior in the order in which they are applied.
> ✓ Each consequence increases in its unpleasantness so that students are motivated to avoid them.
> ✓ Consequences are applied right away, during the day in which the misbehavior occurs. The next day students have a fresh start.

Example

An example of a discipline hierarchy for upper elementary grades (e.g., grades 4 or 5) follows.

Courtesy of Fotolia

> First Infraction – Verbal warning
>
> Second Infraction – Time out
>
> Third Infraction – Time out and behavior sheet
>
> Fourth Infraction – Contact parents
>
> Fifth Infraction – Contact administration
>
> Severe Clause – Contact administration

Teacher and Student Behaviors

The following information identifies your behaviors, as the teacher, and the student behaviors that occur at each level of the discipline hierarchy.

> First Infraction – You desist the student's inappropriate behavior and issue a verbal warning.

Second Infraction – You desist the student's inappropriate behavior and send him/her to a designated spot for time out. The location should be a table or desk with chair set aside for this purpose, and it should be away from the line of vision of other students. The duration of the time out is one minute for each year of the child's age (e.g., nine years old equals nine minutes). If you are concerned about keeping track of the time, a kitchen timer can be set.

Third Infraction – You desist the student's inappropriate behavior and send him/her to the time out desk with an assignment: a behavior sheet. The behavior sheet asks the student to identify what rule was broken and what the student can do to avoid breaking the rule again.

Fourth Infraction – You desist the student's inappropriate behavior and contact his/her parents/guardians. The contact can be via phone, email, a note home that is signed and returned, or an in-person conference. These options afford the opportunity for you to use the most appropriate mechanism for communication. The goal is to inform the parents of their child's misbehavior while asking for their assistance with correcting the problem.

Fifth Infraction – You desist the student's inappropriate behavior and send him/her to the assistant principal in charge of discipline. The assistant principal speaks to the student and determines what should be done. Note: Sending a student to the administration is always the last resort in discipline.

Severe Clause – The severe clause is for a student's misbehavior that is a safety issue such as fighting, throwing furniture, etc. The student must be removed immediately in order to protect your safety and that of your students. Check your school's procedures for handling severe incidents.

9.7

Interventions

Introduction

Sometimes, despite the best plans and preventions, interventions are necessary. Here's a suggested continuum of interventions.

> ❖ In general, interventions should start at the lowest level of the continuum and work upwards. However, there are instances where desisting misbehavior, a higher level intervention, needs to be immediate.
> ❖ Also, be aware, that interactive learners require some "side bar" conversations. These conversations help learners to process the information that they are learning.
> ❖ Side bar conversations may also occur during cooperative learning or problem-based instruction. You will need to judge if these conversations are off topic or distracting and thus warrant intervention.

Low

→ Make eye contact with the student.

→ Stand up if you are seated.

→ Walk toward the student.

→ Walk by the student making eye contact.

   e.g., Use the "teacher look".

→ Stand beside the student.

→ Ask the student a question to redirect behavior.

   e.g., "What do you think?"

→ Touch the student on the upper arm and talk directly to him/her.

   e.g., Ask: "Do you need assistance?"

→ Standing next to the student, desist his/her inappropriate behavior.

→ Talk quietly with the student alone or between classes.

→ Talk to the student in front of the whole class.

High

Desisting Inappropriate Behavior

Steps for Desisting Inappropriate Behavior

Follow these steps to successfully desist a student's inappropriate behavior.

Step 1
Identify the student by name.

Step 2
Tell the student to stop the inappropriate behavior.

Step 3
Identify the rule/procedure being violated or have the student identify the rule/procedure.

Step 4
State the consequence for breaking the rule/procedure according to the discipline hierarchy.

Step 5
State the expected behavior or have the student state the expected behavior.

Step 6
Deliver specific praise/encouragement for the student's expected behavior when displayed.

Courtesy of Fotolia

Example of Desisting Inappropriate Behavior

Scenario

Mrs. Lopez has a classroom management system with colored cards in pockets that track students' daily behavior in her classroom. Each student has a pocket with his/her name on it and four color-coded cards of green, yellow, orange, and red. Green represents good behavior; yellow represents a verbal warning; orange means consequence #2 is implemented; and red means consequence #3 is implemented.

Next to the classroom management system, Mrs. Lopez has posted the classroom rules and consequences, the latter of which are in a discipline hierarchy. The rules are as follow.

1. Show respect to everyone and everything.
2. Always keep your hands, feet, and objects to yourself.
3. Before speaking, raise your hand and wait to be called on.
4. Follow all directions and classroom procedures.
5. Follow all school rules.

The discipline hierarchy of consequences is as follows.

Consequence #1: Verbal warning
Consequence #2: Time out at the back table
Consequence #3: Teacher contacts parents/guardians
Severe Clause: Teacher sends the student to the assistant principal in charge of discipline

The problem is that Michael has called out during Mrs. Lopez's presentation of a lesson. To desist Michael's behavior, the teacher applies the steps to desist behavior by saying the following.

"Michael, please stop calling out." (Steps 1 & 2)
"Remember, rule number three says, 'Raise your hand and wait to be called on before speaking.'" (Step 3)
"This is a verbal warning. Change your card to the color yellow. If you call out again, you will have to change your card to the color orange and have a time out." (Step 4)
"I know that you will raise your hand next time." (Step 5)
"Michael, thank you for raising your hand and following the rules." (Step 6)

Practice Desisting Inappropriate Behavior

Courtesy of Fotolia

Use the rules, consequences, and behavior management system set in the previous scenario to practice desisting a student's behavior for the following incidents.

1. Sarah shoves Tamika when lining up for recess.

2. Juan is tapping his pencil on the desk during a test.

3. Lee is chewing gum in class against school rules.

4. Edward calls Rashid a nasty name as the class is entering the room.

5. Ashley goes to sharpen her pencil in the middle of your lesson, against classroom procedures.

Activity 17: Creating Classroom Rules

Directions:

Review the pages in this module before beginning this activity. In this activity, you will draft classroom rules for your future classroom. Remember to submit the final product to your instructor on the due date.

1. Identify the grade level for your future classroom.

2. Develop and list 3-5 classroom rules.

3. Write a paragraph or two that addresses the following criteria for creating classroom rules.

   I. Practical
      Is each rule developmentally appropriate? Explain why.
   II. Have Rationales
      Is each rule vitally important? Describe why (e.g., focus on safety and instruction).
   III. Well-constructed
      A. Is each rule vitally important?
      B. Are there only about five rules?
      C. Are the rules written in short sentences?
      D. Are the rules written in language that the students can understand?
      E. Are the rules clearly and positively stated (i.e., avoid the use of "no" and "not")?
   IV. Aligned with School Rules
      How do the classroom rules fit with the school's rules?

4. Review and edit your assignment for clarity, accuracy, grammar, and mechanics.

5. Be sure to cite and reference your work.

Activity 18: Creating a Discipline Hierarchy

Directions:

Review the pages in this module before beginning this activity. In this activity, you will draft a discipline hierarchy to use when students misbehave in your future classroom. Remember to submit the final product to your instructor on the due date.

1. Identify the grade level for your future classroom.

2. Develop and list the consequences for your hierarchy. You should have four to five consequences and a severe clause.

3. Describe why the consequences that you have selected are the best consequences for the grade level of your students.

4. Review and edit your assignment for clarity, accuracy, grammar, and mechanics.

5. Be sure to cite and reference your work.

Module 9 References and Sources

Arends, R. I. (2012). *Learning to teach* (9th ed.). New York: McGraw-Hill.

Borich, G. D. (2014). *Effective teaching methods* (8th ed.). Upper Saddle River, NJ: Pearson.

Burden, P. R., & Byrd, D. M. (2013). *Methods for effective teaching: Meeting the needs of all students* (6th ed.). Boston: Allyn & Bacon.

Canter, L., & Canter, M. (1992). *Assertive discipline: Positive behavior management for today's classroom* (2nd ed.). Seal Beach, CA: Lee Canter & Associates.

Charles, C. M. (2014). *Building classroom discipline* (11th ed.). Upper Saddle River, NJ: Pearson.

Curwin, R. L., Mendler, A. N., Mendler, B. D. (2008). *Discipline with dignity: New challenges, new solutions* (3rd ed.). Alexandria, VA: Association for Supervision and Curriculum Development.

Estes, T. H., Mintz, S. L., & Gunter, M. A. (2011). *Instruction: A models approach* (6th ed.) Upper Saddle River, NJ: Pearson.

Emmer, E. T., & Evertson, C. M. (2013). *Classroom management for middle and high school teachers* (9th ed.). Upper Saddle River, NJ: Pearson.

Evertson, C. M., & Emmer, E. T. (2013). *Classroom management for elementary teachers* (9th ed.). Upper Saddle River, NJ: Pearson.

Jackson Hardin, C. (2012). *Effective classroom management: Models and strategies for today's classrooms* (3rd ed.). Upper Saddle River, NJ: Pearson.

Johnson, D. W., & Johnson, R. T. (2013). *Joining together: Group theory and group skills* (11th ed.). Boston: Allyn & Bacon.

Jones, V., & Jones, L. (2013). *Comprehensive classroom management: Creating communities of support and solving problems* (10th ed.). Upper Saddle River, NJ: Pearson.

Scheuermann, B. K., & Hall, J. A. (2012). *Positive behavioral supports for the classroom* (2nd ed.). Upper Saddle River, NJ: Pearson.

Zirpoli, T. J. (2012). *Behavior management: Positive applications for teachers* (6th ed.). Upper Saddle River, NJ: Pearson.

Module 10
Monitoring and Assessment

Defining Monitoring and Assessment

I. What is assessment?

Assessment is the collection and synthesis of information with the purpose of ascertaining the level of students' learning (i.e., knowledge and skills). Assessment is conducted throughout the teaching-learning process for multiple purposes. Examples follow.

When?	Why?
Prior to instruction	To determine what needs to be taught
During instruction	To monitor learning
After instruction	To ascertain if students have met the lesson objectives/standards

II. What is monitoring?

Monitoring is your observation of your students' learning and behavior. These observations will help you to determine if your teaching is promoting the continuous development of students' cognitive, affective, and psychomotor skills. Then, you can adjust instruction accordingly.

III. What are some examples of monitoring tools?

Tools for monitoring are instruments or devices for collecting information on students' knowledge and/or skills during instruction. To monitor students, use some of the teaching strategies and materials discussed in this book as tools.

A. Examples of Teaching Strategies Used for Monitoring

> **Teacher Movement**
> - Walk around the room during the various parts of the lesson in order to observe students' learning and behavior. Sometimes just your presence near students can help them to stay on task. (See Module 8.1 on Methods, Strategies, and Models and Module 9 on Classroom Management.)

> **Brief Assistance**
> - As you walk around the room, stop to briefly assist students who are having difficulty and/or redirect behavior as needed.
> e.g., A student appears to be daydreaming, so you stop and point to the paragraph in the student's textbook where the class is currently reading.

Check for Understanding

- During the lesson, pose questions to assess whether or not your students are comprehending the material that you are teaching. (See Module 8.7 on Discussion and Recitation.)

e.g., What did the Pilgrims value above all else?

e.g., Given our study of eating for healthy living, what connections can you make between diet and obesity?

B. Examples of Materials Used for Monitoring

Worksheets or Workbook Pages

- Having students complete worksheets or workbook pages as part of the lesson will help you to monitor if they are understanding the content that you are teaching.

e.g., Ask your students to complete a crossword puzzle on content-based vocabulary. Reviewing their work will give you an indication of who understands the vocabulary and who needs more assistance with learning.

Manipulatives

- Watching students use manipulatives can help you determine whether or not they are applying the content you are teaching.

e.g., During your lesson on the math concepts of numerators and denominators, observe students' accuracy at using fraction tiles to represent the numerators and denominators in sample fractions. You will be able to determine which students have grasped the concept and which students need more practice.

Technological materials

- Observing students' progress on technological tasks will help you determine their understanding of the content.

e.g., The class is developing a wiki of their content-based vocabulary for the unit on the branches of the U.S. government. By scanning students' entries, you will know what information they understand and in what areas they may need further instruction.

10.1

IV. What are the types of assessment?

A. Traditional Assessment

Traditional assessment refers to **standard methods** that use paper and pencil assignments and/or recitation (i.e., question and answer sessions) to ascertain the level of students' learning.

Courtesy of Fotolia

B. Alternative Assessment

Courtesy of Fotolia

Alternative assessment refers to methods, such as **performance or authentic assessment**, that include things such as demonstrations, projects, plays, etc.

1. **Performance assessment** is a method that has students **physically demonstrate learning** to show mastery.

Examples:

Courtesy of Fotolia

A student completes a lay-up shot on a basketball court to demonstrate mastery of the skill.

A group of students create and sing a rap song about the steps in the scientific method.

Courtesy of Fotolia

2. **Authentic assessment** is a method that has students **physically demonstrate** or apply learning **in a real-life setting** to show mastery.

Examples:

Courtesy of Fotolia

> A student uses lay-up shots on a basketball court during a game to demonstrate mastery of the skill.

> A group of students perform the steps in the scientific method while conducting an experiment.

Courtesy of Fotolia

V. What are some examples of tools for assessment?

Tools for assessment are instruments or devices for collecting information on students' knowledge and/or skills prior to and/or after instruction. Some of the tools listed here are used with traditional assessment, others with performance assessment, and some with both traditional and alternative forms of assessment.

A. Worksheet, Quiz, and Test

- May be paper and pencil or performance assessments, depending on how the tool is structured
- Structure of content varies:
    - ✓ activities such as crossword puzzles, graphic organizers, etc.
    - ✓ quizzes and tests such as multiple choice, fill-in-the blank items, essays, etc.
- Judged for quality by ratings (e.g., 1-5, A-F, etc.)

B. Portfolio

- Collection of a student's work representing knowledge and/or skills
- Piece of work called an artifact or critical task
- Artifact or critical task can be best work only, random samples, or samples of stages of development (e.g., stages of the writing process from brainstorming through final draft)
- May include a grading list or rubric for each artifact or critical task

C. Grading List

- Identification of specific criteria on which the assessment will be judged
- Criteria provide guidance for students on what knowledge and/or skills will be assessed
- Criteria listed on a check sheet

D. Rubric

- Identification of specific criteria on which the assessment will be judged
- Identification of gradations of quality that specify what the student must do to earn specific ratings (e.g., 1-5, A-F, etc.)
- Criteria and gradations of quality provide guidance for students on what knowledge and/or skills will be assessed and how they will be rated
- Can be holistic in nature or specific items rated individually

VI. What makes monitoring and assessment successful?

Successful monitoring and assessment . . .
- are ongoing,
- are examined in light of the standards and objectives for instruction,
- use a variety of methods,
- address students' learning styles,
- accommodate the needs of special populations, and
- promote needed changes in subsequent planning and instruction to improve students' achievement.

Activity 19: Identifying Monitoring Strategies for a Lesson

Directions:

Review the pages in this module and Modules 6 and 7 before beginning this activity. In this activity, you will identify the monitoring strategies that you will use in your lesson. Remember to submit the final product to your instructor on the due date.

1. Identify the grade level of your lesson.
2. List the state standards, goals, and objectives for your lesson.
3. Name and describe the monitoring strategies that you will use.
4. Provide rationales for your selected monitoring strategies (see Module 10.1 for list of items that make monitoring successful).
5. Review and edit your assignment for clarity, accuracy, grammar, and mechanics.
6. Be sure to cite and reference your work.

Activity 20: Identifying Assessments for a Lesson

Directions:

Review the pages in this module and Modules 6 and 7 before beginning this activity. In this activity, you will identify the assessments that you will use in your lesson. Remember to submit the final product to your instructor on the due date.

1. Identify the grade level of your lesson.

2. List the state standards, goals, and objectives for your lesson.

3. Name and describe the assessments that you will use.

4. Identify the type for each selected assessment (i.e., traditional, alternative).

5. Provide a rationale for your choice of assessments (see Module 10.1 for list of items that make assessment successful).

6. Review and edit your assignment for clarity, accuracy, grammar, and mechanics.

7. Be sure to cite and reference your work.

Module 10 References and Sources

Arends, R. I. (2012). *Learning to teach* (9th ed.). New York: McGraw-Hill.

Borich, G. D. (2014). *Effective teaching methods* (8th ed.). Upper Saddle River, NJ: Pearson.

Burden, P. R., & Byrd, D. M. (2013). *Methods for effective teaching: Meeting the needs of all students* (6th ed.). Boston: Allyn & Bacon.

Estes, T. H., Mintz, S. L., & Gunter, M. A., (2011). *Instruction: A models approach* (6th ed.) Upper Saddle River, NJ: Pearson.

McMillan, J. H. (2014). *Classroom assessment: Principles and practice for effective standards-based instruction* (6th ed.). Upper Saddle River, NJ: Pearson.

Module 11
Closure

Tips for Closing a Lesson

What is closure?

Closure provides an ending to a lesson by reviewing and summarizing the content that was covered in the lesson. Select activities to close a lesson that promote students' higher level thinking. These types of activities will help students connect to content in future lessons.

What are some tips for closing a lesson?

Tip 1
Pose questions.
- Ask the students questions that require them to summarize or draw conclusions about the information presented.
e.g., How are the two main characters in the story alike?

Tip 2
Use activities that extend thinking.
- Return to a graphic or advance organizer and have the students summarize the information. (See Module 4 and Module 8.2 for more activity ideas.)
e.g., At the end of a lesson on the Civil War, you might say: "Today we discussed facts about the Civil War. Who wants to share a concept that you identified after completing the organizer?"

Tip 3
Use activities that promote study skills.
- Ask students to share information for a content analysis or concept map.
e.g., After your unit on the causes and effects of European colonization on the Native American tribes of Florida, ask the students to create a concept map for homework that depicts the causes and effects.

Activity 21: Identifying Closing Activities for a Lesson

Directions:

Review the pages in this module and Modules 1.5, 4, and 8.2 before beginning this activity. In this activity, you will identify the assessments that you will use in your lesson. Remember to submit the final product to your instructor on the due date.

1. Identify the grade level of your lesson.
2. List the state standards, goals, and objectives for your lesson.
3. Name and describe the closing activities that you will use.
4. Provide rationales for your selected closing activities. Address the criteria in the following questions.
    A. Are the activities appropriate for the grade level?
    B. Do the activities support learning of the standards, goals, and objectives?
    C. Are the activities usable (i.e., easily accessed/handled, fit the time frame, low cost but high quality?
    D. Will the activities catch your students' attention and maintain motivation?
    E. Do the activities contribute to the variety of activities in the lesson that help address your students' learning styles and accommodate the needs of special populations?
5. Review and edit your assignment for clarity, accuracy, grammar, and mechanics.
6. Be sure to cite and reference your work.

Module 11 References and Sources

Arends, R. I. (2012). *Learning to teach* (9th ed.). New York: McGraw-Hill.

Borich, G. D. (2014). *Effective teaching methods* (8th ed.). Upper Saddle River, NJ: Pearson.

Burden, P. R., & Byrd, D. M. (2013). *Methods for effective teaching: Meeting the needs of all students* (6th ed.). Upper Saddle River, NJ: Pearson.

Estes, T. H., Mintz, S. L., & Gunter, M. A., (2011). *Instruction: A models approach* (6th ed.) Upper Saddle River, NJ: Pearson.

Module 12
Reflection

Defining Reflection

Reflection is an important part of the teaching process. After closing a lesson, you need to reflect on what worked well and what you need to improve for the next time you teach. Once you have completed the reflection, use the information to continuously improve your subsequent teaching. Doing so will make you a **reflective practitioner**.

When reflecting on the successfulness of your lesson, address each component of the lesson plan and its execution. These components are listed below. Then, be sure to use the information for improvement!

1. Instructional materials
2. Set
3. Content
4. Grade level expectations
5. Standards
6. Goals
7. Objectives
8. Accommodations
9. Instructional methods, strategies, and models
10. Classroom management
11. Monitoring
12. Assessment
13. Closure

Courtesy of Fotolia

Activity 22: Practice Reflecting

Directions:

Review the pages in this module before beginning this activity. In this activity you will draft the reflections section for a lesson plan. You may use a lesson that you have taught recently. Or, you may use the lesson plan assignment for this course, if you have had an opportunity to teach it. Remember to submit the final product to your instructor on the due date.

1. Complete the chart below.

2. Write a brief description for each item that summarizes the information in the chart.

Note: You may use the back pages of the activity to write the descriptions. Or, you may type up the descriptions as a Microsoft Word file, print the page, and attach it to the activity.

3. Review and edit your assignment for clarity, accuracy, grammar, and mechanics.

4. Be sure to cite and reference your work.

Criteria	What Worked	What to Improve
1. Instructional materials		
2. Set		
3. Content		
4. Grade level expectations		
5. Standards		
6. Goals		

Criteria	What Worked	What to Improve
7. Objectives		
8. Accommodations		
9. Instructional methods, strategies, and models		
10. Classroom management		
11. Monitoring		
12. Assessment		
13. Closure		

Module 12 References and Sources

Arends, R. I. (2012). *Learning to teach* (9th ed.). New York: McGraw-Hill.

Borich, G. D. (2014). *Effective teaching methods* (8th ed.). Upper Saddle River, NJ: Pearson.

Burden, P. R., & Byrd, D. M. (2013). *Methods for effective teaching: Meeting the needs of all students* (6th ed.). Upper Saddle River, NJ: Pearson.

Estes, T. H., Mintz, S. L., & Gunter, M. A., (2011). *Instruction: A models approach* (6th ed.) Upper Saddle River, NJ: Pearson.